Beyond Absence

Beyond Absence

A Treasury of Poems, Quotations and Readings on Death and Remembrance

COLLECTED BY EDWARD SEARL

Skinner House Books
Boston

ISBN 978-1-55896-492-1

Printed in the United States
Cover art *Memory Blue*, © 2003 Eleanor Rubin, http://ellyrubinjournal.typepad.com
Cover design by Kathryn Sky-Peck
Text design by Dartmouth Publishing, Inc.

22
6 5

We gratefully acknowledge permission for the use of copyrighted text starting on page 213.

Library of Congress Cataloging-in-Publication Data

Beyond absence : a treasury of poems, quotations, and readings on
    death and remembrance / collected by Edward Searl.
      p. cm.
    Includes index.
    ISBN 1-55896-492-4 (alk. paper)
    1. Death—Quotations, maxims, etc. 2. Death—Poetry. I. Searl,
Edward, 1947-   .
    PN6084.D4B49 2005
    808.81'93548--dc22

2005021831

Contents

Dear Reader,

Death, inevitable and necessary, breaks our hearts. Through language we give shape to this heartbreak. The words on these pages, about death and its meaning, are drawn from poets and playwrights, from philosophers and theologians, from clergy and many others for whom death is a familiar presence. The goal of this collection is to offer inspiring and comforting readings that can be woven into a funeral or memorial service, added to a letter of condolence, printed on an order of service, or simply read in privacy. These passages may stimulate your own words should you need to address particular circumstances surrounding dying, grief, or remembrance. You may use this collection as an extended meditation on death's place in the scheme of every human life, including your own.

Throughout the ages, human beings have been understandably ambivalent about death, perhaps never more so than now. In many parts of the world, we sequester those who are elderly or ill. No longer is the body washed at home or laid out in the living room for viewing. We hand over the physical details of death to specialists. When death comes, we may be repulsed, fearful, or simply unprepared. These readings offer a blessed intimacy with an inevitable and defining aspect of human existence.

In my twenty-seven years of ministry, I have found that the right words can make all the difference in comforting those who are grieving the loss of loved ones or confronting the prospect of their own imminent death. I chose these selections with an eye toward the insights of bereavement counseling, which respects the complex and conflicted impact death has on the dying and the ripple effects death has on survivors.

This project humbled me with its gravity and scope. It involves nothing less than the meaning of the human condition. Time and again I was moved by the voice and insight—the measured meaning— of what I read. I felt the empathic embrace of humanity, a great compassion. May it be so for you as well.

Wishing you peace,

Edward Searl

Every Living Hour

Now welcome every living hour;
Delight in every newborn day.
Life is our fame; death has no power
Unless our fear gives death away.

KENNETH PATTON

But this isn't to say that I expect to find peace with death. I still hate it, especially when it comes too soon. But even though I hate it, death also reminds me to treasure life. It reminds me to listen more carefully when my children talk, to call my parents more often, to be patient when the kids are experimenting with all the new ways a piano can be used to make noise. Death reminds me to take chances and risk failure, and it reminds me that I am not alone in the world.

I find solace in celebrating the lives of the people who have come before me. Although I can't say with certainty what will happen to me when I die, I know that I am a part of a great stream of life that began long before I was born and will flow on long after I die. We share immortality in our connections to the universe and through the small, unique ways we change the world as we live in it.

I find sadness and joy in remembering. I also feel anger and comfort. And recognizing these feelings is a part of celebrating. To feel is to be alive, and experiencing our feelings reminds us that life can be filled with meaning, even though death will come to us all someday.

JOEL MILLER

Oh Mother Earth, Father Sky,
Brother Wind, Friend Light, Sweetheart Water,
Here take my last salutation with folded hands!
For to-day I am melting away into the Supreme
Because my heart became pure,
And all delusion vanished,
Through the power of your good company.

HINDU ASCETIC

On no subject are our ideas more warped and pitiable than on death . . . Let children walk with nature, let them see the beautiful blendings and communions of death and life, their joyous inseparable unity, as taught in woods and meadows, plains and mountains and streams of our blessed star, and they will learn that death is stingless indeed, and as beautiful as life, and that the grave has no victory, for it never fights. All is divine harmony.

JOHN MUIR

This then is how we can begin to face death:
by becoming more aware of our fear and seeking courage,
by loving what is mortal, and letting it go when the time comes,
by being present for, and mindful of, every moment of life as well
as our impending death

MICHAEL MCGEE

It is odd that the Bible says, "God created man," whereas it is the other way round: man has created God. It is odd that the Bible says, "The body is mortal, the soul is immortal," whereas even here the contrary is true: the body (its matter) is eternal; the soul (the form of the body) is transitory.

BÉLA BARTÓK

Mother and Father Presence, Spirit of Life,
weaving your love through us and among us:
Comfort us in our sorrows, laugh with us in our joys.
Walk with us as we find the words
or make the pictures
that tell the stories of our lives.
Be a small, still voice in our souls
that calls us to listen, carefully, to the living stories around us;
a small, still voice in our minds
that calls us to an ever greater compassion;
a small, still voice in our hearts
that calls us to cherish all our lives;
a small, still voice in our bodies
that calls us to use our anger to build cities of hope.

Mother and Father of Earth and Stars:
We are all your children. May your love for us
become our own love for all.

Amen. Blessed Be.

JOEL MILLER

The Dead

How great unto the living seem the dead!
How sacred, solemn; how heroic grown;
How vast and vague, as they obscurely tread
The shadowy confines of the dim unknown!—
For they have met the monster that we dread,
Have learned the secret not to mortal shown.
E'en as gigantic shadows on the wall
The spirit of the daunted child amaze,
So on us thoughts of the departed fall,
And with phantasma fill our gloomy gaze.
Awe and deep wonder lend the living lines,
And hope and ecstasy the borrowed beams;
While fitful fancy the full form divines,
And all is what imagination dreams.

CHARLES HEAVYSEGE

A Psalm of Life

Tell me not, in mournful numbers,
    Life is but an empty dream!
For the soul is dead that slumbers,
    And things are not what they seem.

Life is real! Life is earnest!
    And the grave is not its goal;
Dust thou art, to dust returnest,
    Was not spoken of the soul.
Not enjoyment, and not sorrow,
    Is our destined end or way;
But to act, that each to-morrow
    Find us farther than to-day.
Art is long, and Time is fleeting,
    And our hearts, though stout and brave,
Still, like muffled drums, are beating
    Funeral marches to the grave.

In the world's broad field of battle,
    In the bivouac of Life,
Be not like dumb, driven cattle!
    Be a hero in the strife!
Trust no Future, howe'er pleasant!
    Let the dead Past bury its dead!
Act,—act in the living Present!
    Heart within, and God o'erhead!
Lives of great men all remind us
    We can make our lives sublime,
And, departing, leave behind us
    Footprints on the sands of time;

Footprints, that perhaps another,
 Sailing o'er life's solemn main,
A forlorn and shipwrecked brother,
 Seeing, shall take heart again.

Let us, then, be up and doing,
 With a heart for any fate;
Still achieving, still pursuing,
 Learn to labor and to wait.

HENRY WADSWORTH LONGFELLOW

Death is a mirror in which the entire meaning of life is reflected.

SOGYAL RINPOCHE

Death is the mother of beauty, mystical,
Within whose burning bosom we devise
Our earthly mothers waiting, sleeplessly.

WALLACE STEVENS

Life and Death

In the presence
of Life
we say NO
to Death.

In the presence of Death
we say YES
to Life.

J. DONALD JOHNSTON

We are part of the unending cycle of life, and we can take pride and joy in that role. Maybe there is a part of us that unites with the creative force of the universe. If so, not only are our bodies useful after our death but we can take comfort in the thought that the spirit of love that animated us will be recycled as well. The Universe is a closed system. Nothing is wasted. Energy changes to matter and back to energy again. Our death releases the energy stored in our body to be used in another form. Whatever we believe happens to our spirit following our death, the inescapable fact is that we are mortal beings and we will die.

It is worth dying to have lived with such richness. It is worth dying to have experienced the joy of relationships. It is worth dying to have asked such questions and struggled mightily to find the answers. "Living and loving, come what may." To live the cycle of life with courage, honesty, and honor, to participate in the eternal dance of life, this is our fate—and our destiny.

And when death comes calling for a loved one, or for ourselves, may we meet the challenge with courage and dignity. May we overcome despair, set aside irony, and meet our fate bravely. May we never fail to say, "I would not hesitate to choose mortality."

NANA KRATOCHVIL

Death, like birth, is a secret of Nature.

MARCUS AURELIUS

Millions long for immortality who do not know what to do with themselves on a rainy Sunday afternoon.

SUSAN ERTZ

I am of the opinion that my life belongs to the whole community and as long as I live, it is my privilege to do for it whatever I can. I want to be thoroughly used up when I die, for the harder I work the more I live.

GEORGE BERNARD SHAW

Up, sluggard, and waste not life; in the grave will be sleeping enough.

BEN FRANKLIN

Death not merely ends life, it also bestows upon it a silent completeness, snatched from the hazardous flux to which all things human are subject.

HANNAH ARENDT

From too much love of living,
        From Hope and fear set free,
We thank with brief thanksgiving
        Whatever gods may be
That no life lives for ever;
That dead men rise up never;
That even the weariest river
        Winds somewhere safe to sea

ALGERNON CHARLES SWINBURNE

Religion is our human response to the dual reality of being alive and having to die. Knowing that we are going to die, we question what life means. We are not so much the animal with advanced language or the animal with tools as we are the religious animal. Having discovered relics and flowers in ancient graves, certain anthropologists actually apply to us the sobriquet homo religiosus. We have honored our dead from time immemorial, even as we continue to sift through their ashes in anticipation of our own earthly remains.

FORREST CHURCH

Death is the most profound and significant fact of life, raising the least of mortals above the mean commonplaces of life. The fact of death alone gives true depth to the question as to the meaning of life. Life in this world has meaning just because there is death.

NICHOLAS BERDYAEV

How do I know that adoring life is not a delusion? How do I know that we who despise death are not exiled children who don't know their way back?

CHUANG TZU

People living deeply have no fear of death.

ANAÏS NIN

Come lovely and soothing death,
Undulate round the world, serenely arriving, arriving,
In the day, in the night, to all, to each,
Sooner or later delicate death.

Prais'd be the fathomless universe,
For life and joy, and for objects and knowledge curious,
And for love, sweet love—but praise! praise! praise!
For the sure-enwinding arms of cool-enfolding death.

Dark mother always gliding near with soft feet,
Have none chanted for thee a chant of fullest welcome?
Then I chant it for thee, I glorify thee above all,
I bring thee a song that when thou must indeed come, come
    unfalteringly.

Approach strong deliveress,
When it is so, when you have taken them I joyously sing the dead,
Lost in the loving floating ocean of thee,
Laved in the flood of thy bliss, O death.

From me to thee glad serenades,
Dances for thee I propose saluting thee, adornments and feastings
    for thee,
And the sights of the open landscape and the high-spread sky are
    fitting,
And life and the fields, and the huge and thoughtful night.

The night in silence under many a star,
The ocean shore and the husky whispering wave whose voice I know,

And the soul turning to thee O vast and well-veil'd death,
And the body gratefully nestling close to thee.

Over the treetops I float thee a song,
Over the rising and sinking waves, over the myriad fields and the
    prairies wide,
Over the dense-pack'd cities all, and the teeming wharves and ways,
I float this carol with joy, with joy to thee O death!

WALT WHITMAN

The teacher takes a beautiful crystal goblet and says: "Loving this beautiful glass, some people live in fear that someday it will be broken. But the wise person, loving life, knows that the glass is already broken and, thus, drink of life the more deeply."

BUDDHIST PROVERB

We have in life the experience of death, though not the final experience of it. And we cannot be reconciled to death—to the death neither of human beings nor of animals, plants, things or houses. The striving for eternity of all that exists is the essence of life. And yet eternity is reached only by passing through death, and death is the destiny of everything that exists in this world. The higher and more complex a being is, the more it is threatened with death.

The moral paradox of life and of death can be expressed by a moral imperative: treat the living as though they were dying and the dead as though they were alive; i.e., always remember death as the mystery of life and always affirm eternal life in life and in death.

NICHOLAS BERDYAEV

On the World

The world's an Inn; and I her guest.
I eat; I drink; I take my rest.
My hostess, nature, does deny me
Nothing, wherewith she can supply me;
Where, having stayed a while, I pay
Her lavish bills, and go my way.

FRANCIS QUARLES

In becoming forcibly and essentially aware of my mortality, and of what I wished and wanted for my life, however short it might be, priorities and omissions became strongly etched in a merciless light, and what I most regretted were my silences. Of what had I *ever* been afraid?

AUDRE LORDE

Finis

I strove with none, for none was worth my strife.
Nature I loved and, next to Nature, Art:
I warm'd both hands before the fire of life;
It sinks, and I am ready to depart.

WALTER SAVAGE LANDOR

A few can touch the magic string,
    and noisy Fame is proud to win them:—
Alas for those that never sing,
    But die with all their music in them!

OLIVER WENDELL HOLMES

A useless life is an early death.

JOHANN WOLFGANG VON GOETHE

Biological mortality is the only immortality I believe in. It's not a full comfort, I don't suppose, if you're going to come down to a pound and a half of chemicals that will disperse themselves through a lot of other biology, but still it's more comforting than total oblivion. Some people I know take great comfort from the notion of the continuity of life.

WALLACE STEGNER

The laws of life and death are as they should be; and if death ends my consciousness, still is death good. I have had life on those terms, and somewhere, somehow, the course of nature is justified.

I shall not be imprisoned in that grave where you are to bury my body. I shall be diffused in great Nature, in the soil, in the air, in the sunshine, in the hearts of those who love me, in all the living and flowing currents of the world, though I may never again in my entirety be embodied in a single human being. My elements and my forces go back into the original sources out of which they came, and these sources are perennial in this vast, wonderful, divine cosmos.

JOHN BURROUGHS

I had rather think of those I have loved, and lost, as having returned to earth, as having become a part of the elemental wealth of the world—I would rather think of them as unconscious dust, I would rather dream of them as gurgling in the streams, floating in the clouds, bursting in the foam of light upon the shores of worlds, I would rather think of them as the lost visions of a forgotten night, than to have even the faintest fear that their naked souls have been clutched by an orthodox god. I will leave my dead where nature leaves them.

ROBERT INGERSOLL

Since the first human eye saw a leaf in Devonian sandstone and a puzzled finger reached to touch it, sadness has lain over the heart of man. By this tenuous thread of living protoplasm, stretching backward into time, we are linked forever to lost beaches whose sands have long since hardened into stone. The stars that caught our blind amphibian stare have shifted far or vanished in their courses, but still that naked glistening thread winds onward. No one knows the secret of its beginning or its end. Its forms are phantoms. The thread alone is real; the thread is life.

LOREN EISELEY

The winter winds whistle
Across a battered landscape.
Bold. Biting. Boisterous.

They encompass the pain of illness
    and death,

but life continues day by day,
as the scarlet cardinal rests
on my friend's spruce daily.

CAROLYN J. SIBR

Blessed be you, mortal matter: you who one day will undergo the process of dissolution within us and will thereby take us forcibly into the very heart of that which exists.

Without you, without your onslaughts, without your uprootings of us, we should remain all our lives inert, stagnant, puerile, ignorant both of ourselves and of God.

PIERRE TEILHARD DE CHARDIN

In Spring

If I should die (and die I must) please let it be in spring
When I, and life up-budding, shall be one
And green and lovely things shall blend with all I was
And all I hope to be.
The chemistry
Of miracle within the heart of love and life abundant
Shall be mine, and I shall pluck the star-dust and shall know
The mystery within the blade
And sing the wind's song in the softness of the flowered glade.
April is the time for parting, not because all nature's tears
Presage the blooming time of May
But joyous should be death and its adventure
As the night gives way to the day.

GEORGE C. WHITNEY

It is sometimes said that we are born as strangers in the world and that we leave it when we die. But in all probability we do not come into the world at all. Rather we come out of it, in the same way that a leaf comes out of the tree or a baby from its mother's body. We emerge from deep within its range of possibilities, and when we die we do not so much stop living as take on a different form. So the leaf does not fall out of the world when it leaves the tree. It has a different way and place to be within it.

BARBARA HOLLERORTH

I am going out into the Universe to stroll on the Milky Way and bathe in the ocean of Night.

HUGH ROBERT ORR

In a cemetery once, an old one in New England, I found a strangely soothing epitaph. The name of the deceased and her dates had been scoured away by wind and rain, but there was a carving of a tree with roots and branches (a classic nineteenth-century motif) and among them the words, "She attended well and faithfully to a few worthy things." At first, this seemed to me a little meager, a little stingy on the part of her survivors, but I wrote it down and have thought about it since and now I can't imagine a more proud or satisfying legacy.

"She attended well and faithfully to a few worthy things."

Every day I stand in danger of being struck by lightning and having the obituary in the local paper say, for all the world to see, "She attended frantically and ineffectually to a great many unimportant, meaningless details."

VICTORIA SAFFORD

The presence of Death certainly raises existential questions: How did we get here? What is the meaning of our existence? Where were we before birth and what happens to our sense of self after we die? Is this all there is? The illusion, of course, is that Death is not constantly present. When someone close to us dies, we are reminded of the harshness and finality of death, but death has always been with us, walking alongside us.

The first lesson I learned from Death is the finality of loss, that nothing can change things back. The world is turned upside down from one second to the other, especially when death comes as a surprise. We know life is change, that all things are changing all the time, but death is the ultimate change when we lose the people by whom we have measured our lives.

The greatest lesson of Death is that all life is lived in seconds. Until one is truly dead, there is no second that does not hold the fullness of life. Each second holds the infinite possibilities and eternal wonder of life, and therefore, it is precious and to be cherished—an existential gift, continuous and ever-changing. I know that I can cherish one second of life, and then the next, and the next. In time, the measure of my life will change as well, creating new boundaries of self and the ability to love what is lost without so much pain.

SUSAN MANKER-SEALE

I heard a piece on the radio. It was a report from the annual convention of obituary writers in America. I hadn't realized obituary writers had a convention. But the report revealed some interesting things about this particular beat. It turns out that editors from papers like the *New York Times* and *Washington Post* do some actuarial calculations to try to figure out what famous people might be dying in the near future. And on the basis of those predictions, editors assign reporters to interview these "subjects" about their lives and ask them how they want to be remembered. Obituaries are written and filed under lock and key until the appropriate time. Apparently, this is how obituary writers stay ahead of the game.

Most of us will never get the opportunity to have a newspaper reporter come to our homes and solicit the story of our lives. And most of us won't make the obituary page of a national newspaper. But the story of our lives matters deeply too. It matters to us and to our conscience. It matters to those whose lives we touch. To our loved ones. If your faith is like mine and you believe that we all can play a role in shaping the unfolding drama of creation, then the story of our lives matters on an ultimate level, too.

So let us be good and faithful stewards of our lives' stories. Let's pay attention to how the story is unfolding. Go home today and write your obituary as if tomorrow were the last day of your life. Would the story you tell reflect what's most important?

ROBERT HARDIES

It's the little deaths before the final time I fear.
    The blasé shrug that quietly replaces excited curiosity,
    The cynic-sneer that takes the place of innocence,
    The soft-sweet odor of success that overcomes the sense of
        sympathy,
    The self-betrayals that rob us of our will to trust,
    The ridicule of vision, the barren blindness to what was once our
        sense of beauty—
These are deaths that come so quietly we do not know when we
    died.

MAX A. COOTS

Once we faced the threat of personal death and of purposeful apocalypse. Now the dark of the moon between death and rebirth embraces the threat of the death of life itself. In moments of truth, we are aware that all life and all human meaning may suddenly vanish. Yet we must follow the daily path, playing our part, that life and meaning may last, time out of mind.

How can we live this double life? Some cling to faith in a divine plan or in an inexorable law that justifies what is and what will be. Some take refuge in a savior; some in absurdity.

I cannot. I grieve. I ask what part I can play with others to avert everlasting death. I live and savor, work and love. I imagine life into further being. I hope.

GRETA W. CROSBY

Each of us is an artist
Whose task it is to shape life
Into some semblance of the pattern
We dream about. The molding
Is not of self alone, but of shared
Tomorrows and times
We shall never see.
So let us be about our task.
The materials are very precious
And perishable.

ARTHUR GRAHAM

The whole life of the individual is nothing but the process of giving birth to himself; indeed we should be fully born, when we die.

ERICH FROMM

I Will Not Die an Unlived Life

I will not die an unlived life.
I will not live in fear
of falling or catching fire.
I choose to inhabit my days,
To allow my living to open me,
to make me less afraid,
more accessible,
to loosen my heart
until it becomes a wing,
a torch, a promise.
I choose to risk my significance,
to live so that that which came to me as seed
goes to the next blossom,
and that which came to me as blossom,
goes on as fruit.

DAWNA MARKOVA

For simple things that are not simple at all
For miracles of the common way . . .
> Sunrise . . . Sunset
> Seedtime . . . Harvest
> Hope . . . Joy . . . Ecstasy

For Grace that turns
> our intentions into deeds
> our compassion into helpfulness
> our pain into mercy

For Providence that
> sustains and supports our needs

We lift our hearts in thankfulness
> and pray only to be more aware
> and thus more alive.

GORDON B. MCKEEMAN

I've come to think that at the moment of our death we get the big picture. We understand all things—the truth of our families, our choices, our priorities. We see all our fears for what they truly were— silly or right. We have clarity, in an instant, of all that we've stood for, all that we've believed in, all that we've hoped and dreamed and discussed. Great questions about calling and loving and the presence (or absence) of the divine come into sharpest focus. We know, and we take that knowledge into eternity. Whatever it is that we've come to know—the truth of our lives—this we carry into all time. We pray "thank you" indeed, as a guest thanks his host after dinner. We know, as does a guest, that we have been graciously and warmly invited to a table spread with lovely things. We had not earned our invitation; we've just been sensible enough to accept generosity when it is extended. We realize that our participation has come as a gift, not a given. We pray "thank you" to what or whomever we believe will hear us for the opportunity we graciously had to be part of a world of beauty, to have life, to be filled with joy and even agony, to have had our small part in a story that is many thousands of years old. We have had glimpses of truth and beauty. We have found our soul's match in another, and with a shudder or a sigh we have recognized holiness from time to time—we've known it. Yes, our parting mood, as pulse and breathing fade together and end, is not pleading but grateful. We have lived. We are blessed.

ALISON L. BODEN

Human life consists in mutual service. No grief, pain, misfortune, or "broken heart," is excuse for cutting off one's life while any power of service remains. But when all usefulness is over, when one is assured of an unavoidable and imminent death, it is the simplest of human rights to choose a quick and easy death in place of a slow and horrible one.

CHARLOTTE PERKINS GILMAN

We embrace the last question and affirm our last faith:
We acclaim the ending and the void.
We walk without reason into the brightness of life,
And we will step without reasons into the darkness of death.

KENNETH PATTON

Many Winters

All of my life is a dance.
When I was young and feeling the earth
My steps were quick and easy.
The beat of the earth was so loud
That my drum was silent beside it.
All of my life rolled out from my feet
Like my land which had no end as far as I could see.
The rhythm of my life was pure and free.

As I grew older my feet kept dancing so hard
That I wore a spot in the earth.
At the same time I made a hole in the sky.
I danced to the sun and the rain
And the moon lifted me up
So that I could dance to the stars.
My head touched the clouds sometimes
And my feet danced deep in the earth
So that I became the music I danced to everywhere.
It was the music I dance to everywhere
It was the music of life.
Now my steps are slow and hard
And my body fails my spirit.
Yet my dance is still within me and
My song is the air I breathe.
My song insists that I keep dancing forever.
My song insists that I keep rhythm
With all of the earth and the sky.
My song insists that I will never die.

NANCY WOOD

Grant us wisdom, that the sting of transiency may not embitter our
good, but cause us rather to be less careless, more heedful, more
loving throughout our days. May our lives be enriched by the

fleeting joys, the momentary glimpses of beauty, the deeper experiences of love and comradeship we only occasionally fathom— the things of the moment, of the hour, and of the day, which we may treasure and weave into a richer tapestry of memories and meanings.

Grant us to see that only a few things bear the mark of the eternal: the beauty that lives with loving kindness; the truth wrought into the substance of our deeds; the transmutation of suffering into an understanding love; the divine impulse given and received.

And may we so pass through the things that are fleeting as to be richer in the things that abide.

Amen.

JACOB TRAPP

The soul's dark cottage, battered and decayed
Lets in new light through chinks that time has made;
Stronger by weakness, wiser men become,
As they draw near to their eternal home.
Leaving the old, both worlds at once they view,
That stand upon the threshold of the new.

EDMUND WALLER

As we watched the EKG go to flatline,
the family asked me to say a prayer.

I don't remember what I said, but as I closed my eyes
I saw the universe in all its immensity.
I felt both infinitely small and unimaginably huge all at once.
I felt as if I did not have a body, that I was pure spirit.

I had been given a gift there in that room, a taste of what lies
beyond our present reality, always there if we are open to it.

We have all been given a gift. Life.

And we will all be given the gift of death someday,
hopefully only when we are ready.

In between, we can experience the mystery of life through death,
when those we know and love pass over.

RACHELE ROSI-KESSEL

There is a little Sufi story about a stream of water working itself across the country, experiencing little difficulty. It ran around the rocks and through the mountains. Then it arrived at the desert. Just as it had crossed every other barrier, the stream tried to cross this one, but it found that as fast as it ran into the sand its waters disappeared. After many attempts, it became very discouraged.

Then a voice came. "If you stay the way you are you cannot cross the sands; you cannot become more than a quagmire. To go further, you will have to lose yourself."

"But if I lose myself, I will never know what I'm supposed to be."

"On the contrary," said the voice. "If you lose yourself you will become more than you ever dreamed you could be."

So the stream surrendered to the dying sun. And the clouds into which it was formed were carried by the raging wind for many miles. Once it crossed the desert, the stream poured down from the skies, fresh and clean and full of the energy that comes from storms.

If you lose yourself, you will become more than you ever dreamed you could be.

PATRICIA E. DE JONG

I refuse to despair of death. The very fact of death greatly concentrates my soul. We live in its mystery; we work in the dark; we do what we can; we give what we have; we live as we are able. If we cannot solve the riddle, and I wager we cannot, we learn to live with it and enjoy it. So we prepare for death by living a life.

RICHARD S. GILBERT

The Cost

Death is not too high a price to pay
for having lived. Mountains never die,
nor do the seas or rocks or endless sky.
Through countless centuries of time, they stay
eternal, deathless. Yet they never live!
If choice there were, I would not hesitate
to choose mortality. Whatever Fate
demanded in return for life I'd give,
for, never to have seen the fertile plains
nor heard the winds nor felt the warm sun on sands
beside the salty sea, nor touched the hands
of those I love—without these, all the gains
of timelessness would not be worth one day
of living and of loving; come what may.

DOROTHY N. MONROE

It is worthwhile for me to live
And bravely fight for saintly ideals
Although disappointed a thousand times
And perhaps even to fall in this fight
When everything would seem in vain.

Blow, angry winds, through my stony body;
You will not conquer my soul.
I have lived in the center of eternity,
My soul will be eternal.
My living was worth it.

Whoever has been set upon from all sides,
But with his soul has conquered,
Is welcome in the chorus of heroes.
Whoever has broken his shackles
And given wings to his mind
Is marching into a golden future.

Norbert Čapek

In Between

One afternoon some time ago I brought my little baby out to visit a very, very old neighbor who was dying that year, quietly and gracefully, in her gracious home. We were having a little birthday party for her, with sherry and cake and a few old friends gathered round her bed. To free a hand to cut the cake, I put my baby down right on the bed, right up on the pillow—and there was a sudden hush in the room, for we were caught off guard, beholding.

It was a startling sight. There in the late afternoon light were two people side by side, two human merely beings. Neither one could talk, neither one could speak, not in language we could understand, both utterly dependent on the rest of us bustling around, masquerading as immortals. There they were: a plump one, apple-cheeked, a cherry tomato of a babe, smiling; and a silver-thin one, hollow-eyed, translucent, shining, smiling. We revelers were hushed because we clearly saw that these were dancers on the very edge of things. These two were closer to the threshold, the edge of the great mystery, than any of us had been for a long time or would be for a while. Living, breathing, smiling they were, but each with one foot and who knows how much consciousness firmly planted on the other side, whatever that is, whatever that is the starry darkness from whence we come and whither we will go, in time. Fresh from birth, nigh unto death, bright-eyed, they were bookends there, mirrors of each other. Radiant.

Cake in hand, and napkins, knife, glasses, a crystal carafe a century old, we paused there on the thresholds of our own momentary lives.

Then, "What shall we sing?" said someone, to the silence, to the sunlight on the covers, to the stars. It was the only question, then, as now, years later. What on earth shall we sing?

VICTORIA SAFFORD

Brief our days, but long for singing,
When to sing is made our call.
For a million stars now flinging
Light upon this earthly ball.
In a setting of what splendor
Are we given chance to render
Tribute for the whirling sky
Where we live and where we die.

KENNETH PATTON

Teach Us To Number Our Days

So teach us to number our days, that we may apply our hearts unto wisdom.

PSALM 90:12

All that lives must die,
passing through nature to eternity.

WILLIAM SHAKESPEARE

Why is the world so fragile?
Why is the world so enduring?

MARK BELLETINI

The Bird of Time has but a little way
To fly—and Lo! the Bird is on the Wing.

OMAR KHAYYAM

All Things Decay and Die

All things decay with time: The forest sees
The growth and down-fall of her aged trees;
That timber tall, which three-score lustres stood
The proud dictator of the state-like wood,
I mean the sovereign of all plants, the oak,
Droops, dies, and falls without the cleaver's stroke.

ROBERT HERRICK

A Common Destiny

All living substance, all substance
    of energy, being, and purpose,
are united and share the same destiny.

All people,
those we love and those we
    know not of, are united and
    share the same destiny.

Birth-to-death
we share this unity with
the sun,
earth. . .

flowers of the field,
snow flakes,
volcanoes and moon beams.

Birth—Life—Death
Unknown—Known—Unknown

Our destiny: from unknown to unknown.

May we have the faith to
    accept this mystery and build
    upon its ever lasting truth.

DAVID EATON

It is better to go to the house of mourning than to go to the house
of feasting; for this is the end of everyone, and the living will lay it
to heart.

Sorrow is better than laughter, for by sadness of countenance
the heart is made glad.

The heart of the wise is in the house of mourning; but the heart
of fools is in the house of mirth.

ECCLESIASTES 7:2–4

It is true that I'm obsessed with death. I am at every minute attentive to the possibility that in the following hour I will be dead, and the person I am with will say, "I was just in the room with him, and now he is dead." This film is constantly in front of my eyes. Each time I drive back home, which is about once a day, I watch my car getting into an accident, as if I am at a movie theater, and I hear them say, "He just left the crossroad, and then he . . ." I can't avoid watching it. . . .

All my writing is on death. If I don't reach the place where I can be reconciled with death, then I will have failed. If I have one goal, it is to accept death and dying.

Jacques Derrida

Death is sweet when it comes in its time and in its place, when it is part of the order of things.

Antoine de Saint-Éxupéry

All lovely things will have an ending,
All lovely things will fade and die.

Conrad Aiken

In the midst of life we are in death.

BOOK-OF COMMON PRAYER

Living brings you to death, there is no other road.

GALWAY KINNELL

I hope the leaving is joyful and I hope never to return.

FRIDA KAHLO

So you want to live forever, do you? Well, then. Let's freeze the sunset and bore ourselves to death!

RIC MASTEN

There is a Reaper, whose name is Death,
    And, with his sickle keen,
He reaps the bearded grain at a breath,
    And the flowers that grow between.

HENRY WADSWORTH LONGFELLOW

Open the door that opens toward the sky;
Press mind and body hard against this world,
Before we fall asleep, before we die.

JOHN HOLMES

Out of infinity, out of eternity, into time
And on into a future we may not pierce,
Moves a power within us, restless and urging,
Seeking and beyond all that is found, moving on.
Thus out of the unknown, into the unknown,
We come as persons.

ROBERT T. WESTON

They are not long, the weeping and the laughter,
    Love and desire and hate;
I think they have no portion in us after
    We pass the gate.

They are not long, the days of wine and roses:
    Out of a misty dream
Our path emerges for a while, then closes
    Within a dream.

ERNEST DOWSON

All things proceeding from the earth to seasons, all things that lapse
and change and come again upon the earth, these come up from the
earth that never changes, they go back into the earth that lasts forever.

THOMAS WOLFE

You are dust, and to dust you shall return.

GENESIS 3:19

Loss is the price that we pay for living. From the day we are born to the day we die, we are shedding bits and pieces of ourselves as we shape and reshape ourselves, our lives, and our futures. Like a snake that must shed its skin in order to grow, or a bird that must first molt to make room for its new stronger feathers in order to fly, we must let go of parts of ourselves—our identity, our sense of security, and those we love, in order to grow and flourish.

The bad news is that with every loss come pain and anger, grief and sorrow.

The good news is that with every loss come a new beginning and an expanded future.

SYDNEY K. WILDE

This awareness of death is the source of zest for life and of our impulse to create not only works of art, but civilizations as well. Not only is human anxiety universally associated with ultimate death, but awareness of death also brings benefits. One of these is the freedom to speak the truth: the more aware we are of death, the more vividly we experience the fact that it is not only beneath our dignity to tell a lie but useless as well.

ROLLO MAY

Death and dying bring fullness to our lives. This may seem counter-intuitive, for death seems like emptiness and feels like loss, but it is also the fulfillment of something.

Like the relentless descent of winter, the waning sun, and the changing leaves, the fallow fields mark the natural, inevitable, culminating reality of our year, of our lives.

We are given life. And it is taken. There is fullness—in living and in dying.

LYNN THOMAS STRAUSS

Birth and Death

During many lifetimes, birth and death are present,
giving rise to birth and death.
The moment the notion of birth and death arises,
birth and death are there.
As soon as the notion of birth and death dies,
real life is born.

THICH NHAT HANH

We are always saying farewell in this world, always standing at the edge of a loss, attempting to retrieve some human meaning from the silence, something which was precious and is gone.

ADLAI STEVENSON

I believe that the suffering and death of living things is part of a grand and natural cycle, tragic only because we alone among the animals are so aware of mortality and time. Death is not a part of happiness at all, but it makes clear the urgency of joy.

VICTORIA SAFFORD

The Green Door

But I have lived too much to guess of dying
That death's a garden, or to rhyme its fears,
And lived so long—a twelvemonth in a minute—
I think time goes by heartbeats, not by years.

Here in my heart I hold such strong abundance.
I do not care what lies beyond that door.
Life is enough. There is always music,
Always more love, more fun, and always more.

And if the green door opens on tomorrow,
And every friend still answers to his name,
A little death makes eloquent the daylight:
It will be glory that the world's the same.

And we have all been dead, who now are living!
Speak out the secret thing we're certain of:
We're back, we've all come back, we've all been given
A longer time to look, and touch, and love.

And this beloved face of daily living
Lights in a thousand different ways for me,
With brave and starry reasons for not dying:
There is too much to think about, and see. . . .
Though this be wealth I'll never taken to heaven—
High rooms in paneled wood, with beams above,
Slow green surf, a men's choir, flags, wind, running—
This is a chant of praise for things I love:

A long music, and I ask for nothing more
This side the narrow portal, death's green door,

Only to cry with mind and heart and tongue
That death at any age is dying young.

JOHN HOLMES

The bell doth toll for him that thinks it doth; and though it intermit again, yet from that minute that that occasion wrought upon him, he is united to God. Who casts not up his eye to the sun when it rises? But who takes off his eye from a comet when that breaks out? Who bends not his ear to any bell which upon any occasion rings? But who can remove it from that bell which is passing a piece of himself out of this world?

No man is an island, entire of itself; every man is a piece of the continent, a part of the main. If a clod be washed away by the sea, Europe is the less, as well as if a promontory were, as well as if a manor of thy friend's or of thine own were: any man's death diminishes me, because I am involved in mankind, and therefore never send to know for whom the bell tolls; it tolls for thee.

JOHN DONNE

To be courageous about death, we must first recognize and accept that each and every one of us is fearful. We are afraid that we will die, and that our loved ones will die. We are afraid that we will suffer and that we will not be ready when death comes. And we are afraid of what comes after death—if anything.

There is nothing wrong with being afraid of death, as long as we face those fears. That is courage: the ability to face what we fear instead of denying it.

MICHAEL MCGEE

Perhaps the whole root of our trouble, the human trouble, is that we will sacrifice all the beauty of our lives, will imprison ourselves in totems, taboos, crosses, blood sacrifices, steeples, mosques, races, armies, flags, nations, in order to deny the fact of death, which is the only fact we have.

JAMES BALDWIN

Something has spoken to me in the night, burning the tapers of the waning year; something has spoken to me in the night, and told me I shall die, I know not where.

THOMAS WOLFE

> Here in the dark, O heart;
> Alone with the enduring Earth, and Night,
> And Silence, and the warm strange smell of clover;
> Clear-visioned, though it break you; far apart
> From the dead best, the dear and old delight;
> Throw down your dreams of immortality,
> O faithful, O foolish lover!
> Here's peace for you, and surety; here the one
> Wisdom—the truth!—"All day the good glad sun

Showers love and labour on you, wine and song;
The greenwood laughs, the wind blows, all day long
Till night." And night ends all things.

RUPERT BROOKE

When you stop fearing death you can start loving the dead. When you start loving the dead you can forgive the dying. A large part of our anguish in the face of death is the result of things we don't want to let ourselves even feel, much less acknowledge. We're caught in an angry and confused maelstrom of suppressed feelings—and you know what happens to suppressed feelings. They reappear with even more power in different forms. And so we fear death. We fear dying. We even fear the dead.

DON GARRETT

I felt a Funeral, in my Brain,
And Mourners to and fro
Kept treading—treading—till it seemed
That Sense was breaking through—

And when they all were seated,
A Service, like a Drum—
Kept beating—beating—till I thought
My Mind was going numb—

And then I heard them lift a Box
And creak across my Soul
With those same Boots of Lead, again,
Then Space—began to Toll,

As all the Heavens were a Bell,
And Being, but an Ear,
And I, and Silence some strange Race
Wrecked, solitary, here—

And then a Plank in Reason, broke,
And I dropped down, and down—
And hit a World, at every plunge,
And Finished knowing—then—

EMILY DICKINSON

The idea of death, the fear of it, haunts the human animal like nothing else; it is a mainspring of human activity—activity designed largely to avoid the fatality of death, to overcome it by denying in some way that it is the final destiny for man.

ERNEST BECKER

It's almost a cultural taboo to talk openly and honestly about death. We spend a lot of time and energy and money trying to hide the fact of our own mortality.

The problem, of course, is that all this avoidance, all this putting off and postponing is based on a lie. The Buddhist tradition names this lie *avidya,* a fundamental mistakenness about reality and life's impermanence, a lie that leads us astray. The lie makes it hard to separate the important from the unimportant. So much of what might seem all important today may mean nothing at the hour of our death, while those day-to-day life joys we take for granted will mean everything. The retirement plan, the new car, the deadline at work seem so all-important while we have too little time to notice the red cardinal in the dogwood tree or tickle the child or say a morning prayer.

We get it all upside down. We don't even know what our priorities look like anymore. We get caught up in the trivial and transient and turn away from what is eternal.

We don't have all the time in the world.

JAN NIELSEN

Sudden Death and the "To Do" List

Comes the day when life stops.
Sometimes abruptly. Unscheduled. Unplanned.
The calendar full of appointments for tomorrows not to be.
Large things, like tickets bought but not to be used.
Like dinner parties for which invitations have been mailed, responses
    received.
Like speeches scheduled and project deadlines agreed to.
Small things, like clothes at the dry cleaners.
Like a small stack of phone messages to be returned.
Like two lamb chops thawing for tonight's dinner.

No one's Daytimer lists "Death—all day Wednesday" as the final
    appointment.

CYNTHIA B. JOHNSON

Everyone must have two pockets, so that he can reach into the one or the other, according to his needs. In his right pocket are to be the words, "For my sake was the world created," and in his left: "I am earth and ashes."

SIMHA BUNAM

The best of us forever
Escapes, in Love and Song.

JOHN HALL WHEELOCK

Ripening

The longer we are together
the larger death grows around us
How many we know by now
who are dead! We, who were young,
now count the cost of having been.
And yet as we know the dead
we grow familiar with the world.
We, who were young and loved each other
ignorantly, now come to know

each other in love, married
by what we have done, as much
as by what we intend. Our hair
turns white with our ripening
as though to fly away in some
coming wind, bearing the seed
of what we know. It was bitter to learn
that we come to death as we come
to love, bitter to face
the just and solving welcome
that death prepares. But that is bitter
only to the ignorant, who pray
it will not happen. Having come
the bitter way to better prayer, we have
the sweetness of ripening. How sweet
to know you by the signs of this world!

WENDELL BERRY

Sonnet 73

That time of year thou mayst in me behold
When yellow leaves, or none, or few, do hang
Upon those boughs which shake against the cold,
Bare ruin'd choirs, where late the sweet birds sang.

In me thou see'st the twilight of such day
As after sunset fadeth in the west,
Which by and by black night doth take away,
Death's second self, that seals up all in rest.
In me thou see'st the glowing of such fire
That on the ashes of his youth doth lie,
As the death-bed whereon it must expire
Consum'd with that which it was nourish'd by.
This thou perceiv'st, which makes thy love more strong,
To love that well which thou must leave ere long.

WILLIAM SHAKESPEARE

In the great night my heart will go out
Toward me the darkness comes rattling,
In the great night my heart will go out.

OWL WOMAN

There's a certain Slant of light,
Winter Afternoons—
That oppresses, like the Heft
Of Cathedral Tunes—

Heavenly Hurt, it gives us—
We can find no scar,
But internal difference,
Where the meanings are—

None may teach it—Any—
'Tis the Seal Despair—
An imperial affliction
Sent us of the Air—

When it comes, the Landscape listens—
Shadows—hold their breath—
When it goes, 'tis like the Distance
On the look of Death—

EMILY DICKINSON

Like dew drops
on a lotus leaf
I vanish.

SENRYU

This is what age must learn about:
      The ABC of dying.
      The going, yet not going,
      The loving and leaving.
  And the unbearable knowing and knowing.

E. B. WHITE

All Is Dukkha

"All is dukkha," say the Buddhists. I am told that *dukkha* is hard to translate. It means literally "suffering," but the feeling of *dukkha* is closer to impermanence; impermanence is central to the Buddhist path to nirvana, enlightenment.

Dukkha, all is impermanence, nothing lasts. I thought of that yesterday while watching leaves come down in a shower and inhaling the smell of rotting leaves returning to the earth. Leaf to humus and back to earth to nourish the roots of the mother tree. The crows crying as the leaves fall and their nests are exposed—*dukkha*, all is impermanence.

Life goes by, and people who were with us last year at this time have died. All souls pass on, all is *dukkha*, nothing lasts.

The Buddhist path to enlightenment is understanding, accepting impermanence to the point where we no longer struggle against it.

But here in the West we search for that which is permanent even as we live with ceaseless change and uncertainty. We search for a sure footing on the path strewn with fallen leaves; we notice the buds of next year's growth tightly curled and waiting; we hold on to the things we can count on: our church, our community, our memories of those who died before us, our love and hope, and our search for truth in a world that is *dukkha*.

Spirit of creation, Goddess of today—let us find each other in a changing world; let us experience love as something which exists, a possibility which is. Let us know that we are alive and being renewed miraculously each second; that the impermanence gives to life its freshness and surprise; that our memories of yesterday and our expectations of tomorrow make now a cherished, precious, eternal moment.

ELIZABETH TARBOX

What has been plaited cannot be unplaited—
Only the strands grow richer with each loss.

MAY SARTON

Life is too brief
Between the budding and the falling leaf,
Between the seedtime and the golden sheaf,
For hate and spite.
We have no time for malice and for greed;
Therefore with love make beautiful the deed;
Fast speeds the night.

M. VORIES

It is right it should be so:
Man was made for joy and woe;
And when this we rightly know
Through the world we safely go.
Joy and woe are woven fine,
A clothing for the soul divine.
Under every grief and pine
Runs a joy with silken twine.

WILLIAM BLAKE

Empty-handed I entered the world
Barefoot I leave it.
My coming, my going—
Two simple happenings
That got entangled.

KOZAN ICHIKYO

Since tragedy is at the heart of us, go to meet it, work it in to our ends,
instead of dodging it all our days, and being run down by it at last.

WILLIAM JAMES

Because I could not stop for Death,
He kindly stopped for me;
The carriage held but just ourselves
And Immortality.

We slowly drove, he knew no haste,
And I had put away
My labor, and my leisure too,
For his civility.

We passed the school where children played
At wrestling in a ring;
We passed the fields of gazing grain,
We passed the setting sun.

We paused before a house that seemed
A swelling of the ground;
The roof was scarcely visible,
The cornice but a mound.

Since then 'tis centuries; but each
Feels shorter than the day
I first surmised the horses' heads
Were toward eternity.

EMILY DICKINSON

Cowards die many times before their deaths;
The valiant never taste of death but once.
Of all the wonders that I yet have heard,
It seems to me most strange that men should fear;
Seeing that death, a necessary end,
Will come when it will come.

WILLIAM SHAKESPEARE

Life is an incurable disease.

ABRAHAM COWLEY

November

How senseless to dread whatever lies before us
when, night and day, the boats,
strong as horses in the wind,
come and go,

bringing in the tiny infants
and carrying away the bodies of the dead.

BILLY COLLINS

We may look at an autumn tree so beautiful in its brilliant colors that we feel like weeping; or we may hear music so lovely that we are overcome with sadness. The craven thought then creeps into our consciousness that maybe it would have been better not to have seen the tree at all or not to have heard the music. Then we wouldn't be faced with this uncomfortable paradox—knowing that "time will come and take my love away," that everything we love will die. But the essence of being human is that, in the brief moment we exist on this spinning planet, we can love some persons and some things, in spite of the fact that time and death will ultimately claim us all.

ROLLO MAY

Snatching the eternal out of the desperately fleeting is the great magic trick of human existence.

TENNESSEE WILLIAMS

Sleep will come upon our eyelids
And they will not ever be lifted again.
Our dreams will be dust with the lost
Dust of our anonymous bones.
The soil that bred us will nourish others
Beneath sun and moon and indifferent stars
For no one knows how many ages to come.

JACOB TRAPP

Ashes to ashes,
dust to dust,
memory to memory,
story to story,
blessing to blessing,
strength to strength,
gratitude to gratitude,
spirit to spirit
love to love.
The wheel turns ever,
and what came out of the earth
returns to it now in peace.

MARK BELLETINI

The passing moments of life flame and fall like the leaves on the maple trees. Our lives, too, flame briefly and fall when seen against the vastness of space-time. If any one of us were to die today, or lose a loved one today, it would be too soon. There is no altering that reality. Yet our lives have extended back before we were born and they will echo long after we are gone. We cannot have an infinite number of years, yet we can choose to let the quality and deeds of our lives echo on and on and on. Who can be sure how long our having been here will reverberate?

ANN E. TYNDALL

We learn from the dying to remember that we are all dying. Dancing the acceptance of our death, we can dance more freely in our lives. Putting death at the center of our lives, not hiding it away in denial and focusing on the trivial, we put life at the center of our lives. Admitting our solidarity as humans vulnerable to illness and death, we become humans capable of true communion with one another in authentic relationship. Living in the present moment, filled with gratitude for one another and bequeathing our life's story to love's eternity, we stay closer to the life for which we yearn. So we pray, on this day, of poignant autumn, to live as if this is our last day before we enter the mystery of death.

KATHLEEN HEPLER

And I drew too the way my father once looked at a bird lying on its side against the curb near our house. It was Shabbos and we were on our way back from the synagogue.

"Is it dead, Papa?" I was six and could not bring myself to look at it.

"Yes," I heard him say in a sad and distant way.

"Why did it die?"

"Everything that lives must die."

"Everything?"

"Yes."

"You, too, Papa? And Mama?"

"Yes."

"And me?"

"Yes," he said. Then he added in Yiddish, "But may it be only after you live a long and good life, my Asher."

I couldn't grasp it. I forced myself to look at the bird. Everything alive would one day be as still as that bird?

"Why?" I asked.

"That's the way the Ribbono Shel Olom made His world, Asher."

"Why?"

"So life would be precious, Asher. Something that is yours forever is never precious."

CHAIM POTOK

"Death is our eternal companion," don Juan said with a most serious air. "It is always to our left, at an arm's length. It was watching you when you were watching the white falcon; it whispered in your ear

73

and you felt its chill, as you felt it today. It has always been watching you. It always will until the day it taps you." . . .

"The thing to do when you're impatient," he proceeded, "is to turn to your left and ask advice from your death. An immense amount of pettiness is dropped if your death makes a gesture to you, or if you catch a glimpse of it, or if you just have the feeling that your companion is there watching you."

CARLOS CASTANEDA

We don't ever totally understand an act such as this—the taking of one's own life. Suicide is a hard word to say. But we must say it, so that in time we can accept it. And even in the midst of our grief we can respect it as a choice—some say the ultimate choice of self-determination. This respect doesn't come easily but it can break upon us like sunlight shafting through a troubled sky.

We can't relinquish our grief totally, but let's put it aside as best as we can, if only briefly. Let us be mindful of our companion, whose death faces us now—a unique personality to be remembered for all his years and not just his final choice.

A person is not just one moment or even a few moments, rather the sum of all moments. Let us not objectify our companion by remembering him for the choice he made to end his life. Let us strive to remember the whole person who lived.

EDWARD SEARL

Death is truly a mystery. We know some things, we believe others. But in the end, it is a mystery. Much of coming to terms with our own death is learning to accept this mystery. These days, in our modern world of information overload and our tremendous breadth of technological and scientific knowledge, we are no longer accustomed to mystery.

I believe that coming to terms with death means acknowledging that we cannot know what will happen to us. It is uncomfortable for us—this not knowing. But it is also real.

And if we can truly accept the mystery of death, we become free to accept the mysteries of life.

Grace lives in that mystery, grace that surprises us with love when we are lonely, with beauty when we are in pain, with life in the midst of death.

REBECCA F. BENNER

The double destiny of being human
is to sense the brevity; compare life to
a candle, to the grass;
but also to sense the length,
the breadth and depth,
the continued story
that the sense of brevity enriches.

J. DONALD JOHNSTON

What Does Death Teach Us About Living?

We know
    That time defines our limit
    Even as eternity expresses our hope.
We know
    that life—
    mine and yours and ours—
    is the tension
    of time
    and eternity,
    and that
    death
    is the resolution. . . .
Our knowledge
    our ignorance,
    our fear
    of death
    leaves us in truth
    with only one clear choice:
    to choose what we shall do
    and be
    in the limited time we have;
    to create ourselves
    within the structures of human existence
        dying as we live,
        living as we die. . . .

What we know
    is that death is natural,
    a biological phenomenon
    related
    to the very complexity
    that is the source
    of our uniqueness
    as a life form;
    such a complicated structure
        as the human being
            breaks down in time;
        that we know
            without doubt
            and without exception. . . .
The acceptance
    of death
    intensifies
    our awareness
    of life,
    makes
        each flower
        and bird
        and mountain,
        each artifact of life,
        more precious
        and more beautiful,

becomes a spur to us
to make something
    lovely and
    meaningful
    of the life that is ours. . . .
To spend ourselves completely
  enables us to know
    a sense of fulfillment,
    a sense of having really lived. . . .
    which help us to overcome
    our fears
    of death
    and dying,
    our frustrations
    at life's brevity,
    our bewilderment
    at our fate. . . .
We are each unique,
  but we are not ultimately alone;
  what we do matters
    to ourselves,
    to the people in our lives,
    to the planet that is our home,
    even to the stars in their courses.
The acceptance
  of death

is grounded
in the knowledge
that we are connected
in life
and in death
to each other
and to every being.

KENNETH W. PHIFER

The Village Atheist

Ye young debaters over the doctrine
Of the soul's immortality
I who lie here was the village atheist,
Talkative, contentious, versed in the arguments
Of the infidels.
But through a long sickness
Coughing myself to death
I read the *Upanishads* and the poetry of Jesus.
And they lighted a torch of hope and intuition
And desire which the Shadow,
Leading me swiftly through the caverns of darkness,
Could not extinguish.
Listen to me, ye who live in the senses

And think through the senses only:
Immortality is not a gift,
Immortality is an achievement;
And only those who strive mightily
Shall possess it.

EDGAR LEE MASTERS

The Last Year

This is the last year.
There will be no other,
but heartless nature
seemingly relents.
Never has a winter sun
spilled so much light,
never have so many flowers
dared such early bloom.
The air is brilliant, sharp.
Never have I taken
such long, long breaths.

ROBERT FRIEND

End Line (for Jim Fulks)

I've always been
a yin/yang—front/back—clear/blur
up/down—life/death kind of guy
my own peculiar duality being
philosopher slash hypochondriac
winwin characteristics
when you've been diagnosed
with advanced prostate cancer

finally the hypochondriac
has more than windmills to tilt with
the philosopher arming himself
with exactly the proper petard
an explosive statement
found in an e-mail message
beneath the signature
of a cancer survivor's name
a perfect end line wily and wise
quote: I ask God:
"How much time do I have before I die?"
"Enough to make a difference,"
God replies.

RIC MASTEN

We Are Those Who Mourn

God of tears and mysterious silence, God of suffering and God of hope, you have made for everything a season. This is the season of our sorrow, and we pray for grace to deal with what seems impossible. We remember the promise made to those who mourn, yet too often it seems that comfort is beyond our grasp. We know that we cannot bear this burden alone. Should we pray for our grief to be transformed or, is the purpose of our grief to transform us? Will our sorrow lead somewhere unexpected? Might it lead us back to life if we follow it? Is it a reminder of the precious reality of life and love? The death of our loved one has created a vast, empty space within our lives, a great longing within our hearts. Can it ever be filled? Can it be healed by the sacred memory that makes our loved one forever a part of us?

So many questions, O God, and so much silence. May we be patient toward all that is unanswered in our hearts. And may others be patient with us, with our sorrow, our anger, our fear, and our questions. We are those who mourn. We seek the comfort that we can offer each other and the blessings of divine love and grace.

Amen.

KIRK LOADMAN-COPELAND

Give sorrow words; the grief that does not speak
Whispers the o'er-fraught heart and bids it break.

WILLIAM SHAKESPEARE

To live is to suffer. To survive is to find meaning in the suffering.

VIKTOR FRANKL

To have suffered much is like knowing many languages. Thou has
learned to understand all.

GEORGE ELIOT

This morning
every memory about you is grief.

BARBARA PESCAN

There's little joy in life for me,
And little terror in the grave;
I 've lived the parting hour to see
Of one I would have died to save.

CHARLOTTE BRONTË

The night wind sighs and whispers
As if it were distressed;
The gusty rain is rattling
My window to the west.
I toss and wake from dreaming,
While dead leaf over leaf
Is joining in the courtyard
The autumn song of grief.

KENNETH PATTON

One common way of marking the passing of loved ones is to have a memorial service, which often helps to begin a healthy process of grieving. I learned to think about a memorial service as a three-act play.

The first act consists of recognizing and acknowledging the loss suffered.

The second act involves remembering and celebrating the life of the deceased.

And finally, in the third act, we reflect on where we go from here. How do we come to terms with the fact that life must go on?

MARK W. HAYES

The gravesite's finality never fails to elicit blocked tears.

ERICA JONG

Elegy

Since I lost you, my darling, the sky has come near,
And I am of it, the small sharp stars are quite near,
The white moon going among them like a white bird among
    snow-berries,
And the sound of her gently rustling in heaven like a bird I hear.

And I am willing to come to you now, my dear,
As a pigeon lets itself off from a cathedral dome

To be lost in the haze of the sky, I would like to come,
And be lost out of sight with you, and be gone like foam.

For I am tired, my dear, and if I could lift my feet,
My tenacious feet from off the dome of the earth
To fall like a breath within the breathing wind
Where you are lost, what rest, my love, what rest!

D. H. LAWRENCE

Out of their sorrow shall come understanding,
Through suffering they are joined with all who live.

STANTON COIT

Each time a person I have treasured dies, a little bit of me dies as
well. I wonder if this isn't nature's way of easing my own death.
There will be so little to give up.

DONALD H. WHEAT

Grief has its beginnings in the twin necessities of attachment and separation. There is no life without either attachment or loss; hence there is no life without grief. And when attachments are strong and deep, the feelings of loss that accompany separation are strong as well.

MARK W. HAYES

Let's talk of graves, of worms, and epitaphs;
Make dust our paper, and with rainy eyes
Write sorrow on the bosom of the earth.

WILLIAM SHAKESPEARE

How can I rest? How can I be at peace? Despair is in my heart. What my brother is now, that shall I be when I am dead . . . I have wept for him day and night, I would not give up his body for burial, I thought my friend would come back because of my weeping. Since he went, my life is nothing.

THE EPIC OF GILGAMESH

Too Soon

In my note to him, dying, I wrote:
   "I saw some warblers in the yard.
   It seems too soon."

He knew about warblers
and when it was time for them to go.
Did he know also that I was saying,
   "It's too soon for you to die?"

He was young. He was good.
He was wise. He was giving.

I saw some warblers.
He has died.
Why, God,
   do some things come too soon?

SUZANNE REININGA

With you a part of me hath passed away;
For in the peopled forest of my mind
A tree made leafless by this wintry wind
Shall never don again its green array. . . .

Chapel and fireside, country road and bay,
Have something of their friendliness resigned;
Another, if I would, I could not find,
And I am grown much older in a day.

But yet I treasure in my memory
Your gift of charity, and young heart's ease,
And the dear honor of your amity;
For these once mine, my life is rich with these.
And I scarce know which part may greater be,—
What I keep of you, or you rob from me.

GEORGE SANTAYANA

The bustle in a house
The morning after death
Is solemnest of industries
Enacted upon earth.

The sweeping up the heart
And putting love away
We shall not want to use again
Until eternity.

EMILY DICKINSON

Not people die but worlds die in them.

YEVGENY YEVTUSHENKO

Good-Night

Good-night! . . . my darling sleeps so sound
She cannot hear me where she lies;
White lilies watch the closed eyes,
Red roses guard the folded hands.

Good-night! O woman who once lay
Upon my breast, so still, so sweet
That all my pulses, throbbing, beat
And flamed—I cannot touch you now.

Good-night, my own! God knows we loved
So well, that all things else seemed slight—
We part forever in the night,
We two poor souls who loved so well.

MARY GILMORE

Your logic, my friend, is perfect,
    Your moral most drearily true;
But, since the earth clashed on her coffin,
    I keep hearing that, and not you.

Console if you will, I can bear it;
    'Tis a well-meant alms of breath;
But not all the preaching since Adam
    Has made Death other than Death.

JAMES RUSSELL LOWELL

Three Haiku

lingering
over the empty bowl—
an echo

bare trees
stark against the twilight sky—
silence

one seated
at a table for two—
shadows lengthen

JOSEPH KIRSCHNER

Who do the dead think they are!
Up and dying in the middle of the night
leaving themselves all over the house,
all over my books, all over my face?
How dare they sit in the front seat of my car,
invisible, not wearing their seat belts,
not holding up their end of the conversation,
as I drive down the highway
shaking my fist at the air all the way
to the office where they're not in.
The dead get by with everything.

BILL HOLM

I am not here to tell you how to take away the pain of such loss. I
wouldn't even if I could, for this kind of pain is as much an expression
of love as laughter and joy. No. The way to face the death of a loved

one does not go through pretending that it does not hurt, or that the loss is somehow less than it is. The way goes through something else, something that begins in tears and anguish. It begins in the stark recognition that this person whom we have loved and cherished and treasured for years is—or will soon be—no longer among us. It begins with the honest acceptance of the fact that such absolute absence hurts.

KENNETH W. COLLIER

Your absence has gone through me
Like thread through a needle.
Everything I do is stitched with its color.

W. S. MERWIN

For the first sharp pangs there is no comfort—whatever goodness may surround us, darkness and silence still hang about our pain. But slowly, the clinging companionship with the dead is linked with our living affections and duties, and we begin to feel our sorrow as a solemn initiation, preparing us for that sense of loving, pitying fellowship with the fullest human lot, which, I think, no one who has tasted it will deny to be the chief blessedness of our life. And especially to know what the last parting is, seems needful to give the utmost sanctity of tenderness to our relations with each other.

GEORGE ELIOT

Sorrow makes us all children again,—destroys all differences of intellect. The wisest know nothing.

RALPH WALDO EMERSON

Let grief be your sister, she will whether or no.
Rise up from the stump of sorrow, and be green also,
like the diligent leaves.

MARY OLIVER

Isn't it strange that one of the ways we comfort those who are undergoing grief and sorrow is to remind them of others who have had the same misfortune, as if their pain was not great enough.

We act as though one sorrow will rule out another. If ever there was a time when we have the right to be unique and special, it is in the time of tragedy. The Old Testament words "if there is any sorrow like my sorrow" are their special right.

Donald H. Wheat

May we not be spared those sufferings that come to all who think and feel. May we never be indifferent to another's pain. Give us to choose suffering rather than insensitivity, the riches of compassion rather than the poverty of living apart from others. Lead us through the door of our common sorrows into the many mansioned house of understanding.

May the comfort of those who give comfort to others be ours; and the glad homecoming of those who, although have sown in tears, bore precious seed, and return rejoicing, bringing their sheaves with them.

Jacob Trapp

I have learned that a single human life is the most precious entity in all of God's creation, not to be bartered for a genie's wish or a king's fortune.

I have learned that our abundant existence on earth
is too much filled with petty thoughts, trivial
concerns, and a meanness toward our fellow creatures.

I have learned that it is good to live with a knowledge of
our finitude, as if each moment is our last, so that
what we do is a new kind of doing.

I have learned that our fear of death, which arises
from our personal fantasies and cultural anxieties,
is more to be dreaded than death itself.

And I have also learned that the human being is a
marvelous construction, with the faith and courage
to confront any power in the universe—even the reaper,
whose name is Death.

DAVID O. RANKIN

The best thing we can do for a bereaved person is to companion
them—to be truly present with humility, knowing that you will learn
from them. Allow yourself to be vulnerable. Attend the memorial
service. Call to ask how they are in the weeks and months that
follow. Perhaps it's difficult to know what to say. Don't struggle with

that. Just say something like "How are you in these difficult times?" Be open to any response. You might respond, "I'm so very sorry." You don't have to stay long. This is enough.

If the person wants to talk, just listen with your heart; affirm their words. It's okay to shed tears with them to share their mourning. Don't forget them as the weeks and months go by. Remember their anniversaries and holiday celebrations. Write notes and cards. Notice whether they need help with cleaning the house or cooking meals. Sadness is exhausting.

Offer to meet them and be prepared to hear the same stories again and again. Be open to reports of mystical experiences. Appearance of the deceased is extremely common within the first six months following the death of a loved one. Sometimes the person may just feel the "presence" in the house. Do not judge this. These appearances are a great comfort to the bereaved.

Don't be surprised if the bereaved person experiences sadness, numbness, depression, confusion, yearning, and outbursts of emotion, even panic, as the grief comes in waves. If it seems to you that the person is in danger, suggest that because you care a great deal you wish he or she would see a professional.

There are a few don'ts: Don't use clichés like "Time heals all wounds." Don't advise them to get busy! These words deny their grieving and mourning process. Just walk with them, companion them, in their grief.

ANN C. FOX

What is there to say about grief?

Grief is a tidal wave that overtakes you, smashes down upon you with unimaginable force, sweeps you up into its darkness, where you tumble and crash against unidentifiable surfaces, only to be thrown out on an unknown beach, bruised, reshaped.

Grief means not being able to read more than two sentences at a time. It is walking into rooms with intention that suddenly vanishes.

Grief is three-o'clock-in-the-morning sweats that won't stop. It is dreadful Sundays, and Mondays that are no better. It makes you look for a face in a crowd, knowing full well the face we want cannot be found in that crowd.

Grief is utter aloneness that razes the rational mind and makes room for the phantasmagoric. It makes you suddenly get up and leave in the middle of a meeting, without saying a word.

Grief makes what others think of you moot. It shears away the masks of normal life and forces brutal honesty out of your mouth before propriety can stop you. It shoves away friends, scares away so-called friends, and rewrites your address book for you.

Grief makes you laugh at people who cry over spilled milk, right to their faces. It tells the world that you are untouchable at the very moment when touch is the only contact that might reach you. It makes lepers out of upstanding citizens.

Grief discriminates against no one. It kills. Maims. And cripples. It is the ashes from which the phoenix rises, and the mettle of rebirth. It returns life to the living dead. It teaches that there is nothing absolutely true or untrue. It assures the living that we know nothing for certain. It humbles. It shrouds. It blackens. It enlightens.

Grief will make a new person out of you, if it doesn't kill you in the making.

STEPHANIE ERICSSON

Grief can awaken us to new values and new and deeper appreciations. Grief can cause us to reprioritize things in our lives, to recognize what's really important and put it first. Grief can heighten our gratitude as we cease taking the gifts life bestows on us for granted. Grief can give us the wisdom of being with death. Grief can make death the companion on our left who guides us and gives us advice.

None of this growth makes the loss good and worthwhile, but it is the good that comes out of the bad.

ROGER BERTSCHAUSEN

As the stages of grief pass through the heart like electric shocks— painful and powerful—the person who was alive and loved among us is transformed into someone loved and yet among us in a different way. It is such a mystery that every human culture has made up amazing stories to explain and contain it, and yet it remains a mystery—inspiring terror and wonder. It is in inescapable mystery that transforms all of life, that is woven into life.

We gently, quietly tear up at funerals and then go somewhere to be alone and cry out our private sorrow—our sorrow which is not truly private at all. It is the other secret we all share. We sorrow and grieve.

It's this grieving that begins to clear out the heart—and allows in the reality of loss in. It allows the heart to heal and let life return— a new and different life, but a real one. At some point, ready or not, we each have a standing invitation to meet with mortality. If we are wise we become more fully alive at that moment. We don't cling feverishly to life but we cherish the lives of others because they, too, are such brief and remarkable occurrences.

HILARY LANDAU KRIVCHENIA

Remembering well means grieving well, and grieving well means getting from anger and fear and guilt and despair to blessing. It means giving sorrow words, or music, or dance, or ritual or some other expression. It means feeling the pain, not so that you can keep it, but so that you can let it go.

SARAH YORK

Talking to Grief

Ah, Grief, I should not treat you
like a homeless dog
who comes to the back door
for a crust, for a meatless bone.
I should trust you.

I should coax you
into the house and give you
your own corner,
a worn mat to lie on,
your own water dish.

You think I don't know you've been living
under my porch.
You long for your real place to be readied
before winter comes. You need
your name,
your collar and tag.
You need
the right to warn off intruders,

to consider
my house your own
and me your person
and yourself
my own dog.

DENISE LEVERTOV

Suffering makes one more sensitive to the pain in the world. It can teach us to put forth a greater love for everything that exists. . . . What is essential is whether we carry out the act of suffering or are acted upon, indifferent as stones. What matters is whether the suffering becomes our *passion*, in the deep double sense of that word. The act of suffering is then an exercise, an activity. We work with suffering. We perceive, we express ourselves, we weep.

DOROTHEE SOELLE

Grieving is hard, some of the hardest work we do, and too often we find ourselves trying to take a shortcut, aided and abetted by our grief-avoiding culture. Yet we cannot shortcut the process. We cannot deny grief its due, or we'll find ourselves losing wallets, or worse, misplacing our sense of selves.

And we are never truly done with grieving. Each loss we have brings back the ones that have come before. When we learn something new about ourselves, or about that which is lost, or about our relationship to that which is lost, we go back again and reevaluate everything in the light of that new information. We revisit the old hurts, the old haunts, looking again for the ways in which we can transform, not transcend, grief. We must, always, be able to know what is lost before we can truly see what is left, and how that might be transformed.

LISA PRESLEY

I share with you the agony of your grief,
    The anguish of your heart finds echo in my own.
    I know I cannot enter all you feel
    Nor bear with you the burden of your pain;
I can but offer what my love does give:
    The strength of caring,
    The warmth of one who seeks to understand
    The silent storm-swept barrenness of so great a loss.
This I do in quiet ways,
    That on your lonely path
    You may not walk alone.

HOWARD THURMAN

He talked to her of the great waste of years between then and now. A long time gone. And it was pointless, he said, to think how those years could have been put to better use. . . . there was no recovering them now. You could grieve endlessly for the loss of time and for the damage done therein. For the dead and for your own lost self. But what the wisdom of the ages says is that we do well not to grieve on and on . . .you can grieve your heart out and in the end you are still where you were. All your grief hasn't changed a thing. What you have lost will not be returned to you. It will always be lost. You're left with only your scars to mark the void. All you can choose to do is go on or not. But if you go on, it's knowing you carry your scars with you.

IAN FRAZIER

Joyfully participate in the sorrows of life.

BUDDHIST BLESSING

Every tear we shed is a midwife which helps bring us into a new world.

KENNETH L. COHEN

The Goddess of Mercy has a thousand hands, and needs them all.

JAPANESE PROVERB

Remember Me

Remember me when I am gone away,
　　Gone far away into the silent land;
　　When you can no more hold me by the hand,
Nor I half turn to go, yet turning stay.
Remember me when no more day by day
　　You tell me of our future that you plann'd:
　　Only remember me; you understand
It will be late to counsel then or pray.
Yet if you should forget me for a while
　　And afterwards remember, do not grieve:
　　For if the darkness and corruption leave
　　A vestige of the thoughts that once I had,
Better by far that you should forget and smile
　　Than that you should remember and be sad.

CHRISTINA ROSSETTI

Sonnet 3

When to the Sessions of sweet silent thought
I summon up remembrance of things past,
I sigh the lack of many a thing I sought,
And with old woes new wail my dear time's waste:
Then can I drown an eye, unused to flow,
For precious friends hid in death's dateless night,
And weep afresh love's long-since-cancell'd woe,
And moan th' expense of many a vanish'd sight:
Then can I grieve at grievances foregone,
And heavily from woe to woe tell o'er
The sad account of fore-bemoanèd moan,
Which I new pay as if not paid before.
But if the while I think on thee, dear friend,
All losses are restored and sorrows end.

WILLIAM SHAKESPEARE

The poet Keats once wrote, "Do you not see how necessary a world of pains and troubles is, to school an intelligence and make it a soul?" This is the opportunity death offers all those who mourn—it is an occasion for growing your soul.

We don't understand. We don't know. But as we are tumbled down the stream of life, so we are worn down, smoothed out, and we discover how necessary a world of pains and troubles is. We learn that losses can become opportunities for greater understanding; they can create the room in us for other people's grief. We learn that letting go of things we have held fast gives us the freedom to move, to fly, to soar. We learn that in loneliness we can seek and find other souls. And some of us, as we are tumbled down the river of life, can begin to understand that the mountain never lets us go. We are part of it; the mountain is in us, over us, and around us all the time. However small a stone, and however tumbled we may be, we are part of the mountain, always.

Each passage into death is unique and has its own story. They say that people die as they live. I would say that is true, sometimes. They say a lot of things about death. It's the great mystery we wonder about, knowing we shall all experience it one day. But what is so very important is that we honor the process. It's one of life's major passages; it is unique and a journey we can prepare for, just as we prepare for the birth of a child.

We are tumbled down the mountain, and we are worn away. We are transformed in the process, both the dying and the bereaved. May we remember that death and bereavement are both opportunities for growing our souls.

MARGOT CAMPBEL GROSS

In the legacies of the dead, we find the seeds of life. In our unfinished business with those we love, we find the core of ourselves.

KRISTA TAVES

What I really wanted was to go to a loud bar and get drunk and smoke cigarettes and laugh. I wanted food and loud music and bodies holding each other close. I wanted to forget all about small white coffins and raw holes in the ground and mothers on their knees crying. I was embarrassed by my intense desires. It would be a long time before I began to understand that for me, desire was the pull back to life and I needed to follow it. It would be a long time before I learned to respect and listen to my body's craving for the pleasure in the face of loss, before I understood that it is all right, even good, to remind myself, after I have stood close to death once again, that I am still alive.

ELEA KEMLER

The logarithms of love and death are riddled with paradox. The more you love the more you risk to lose and therefore stand to fear. Yet love casts out all fear. The greater your love the deeper your grief at a time of loss. Therefore, grief is good. The heart of Christianity is broken and saved by such a paradox. Empty yourself and be filled, Jesus taught. Lose yourself and be found. In the Christian mythos, Jesus died that we might live.

God may not be love. God may not be, who knows, but something is, something bigger than any word, any concept, any doubt, or any creed. All we know is this: Whether God is love or not, love is divine. Nothing else matters. Only love and death.

FORREST CHURCH

The south-wind brings
Life, sunshine, and desire,
And on every mount and meadow
Breathes aromatic fire;
But over the dead he has no power,
The lost, the lost, he cannot restore;
And, looking over the hills, I mourn
The darling who shall not return.

RALPH WALDO EMERSON

No one can quite know your grief and anguish,
though like anguish has been felt,

like questions asked,
even like curses spit into an empty sky.
We can stroke the arm and murmur yes, yes,
sit hour by hour, pour our condolences out like bathing fountains.
Your grief is yours alone—
it will do to you what it may
if you will not make of it what you can.

PATRICK MURFIN

The wisdom of shiva etiquette is striking. When people visit someone sitting shiva, they are supposed to enter quietly and take a seat near the mourner. Then they are to remain silent until the mourner addresses them first. This etiquette recognizes the complexity of grief. It understands that none of us can know exactly what the mourner most needs at any moment. It might be a listening ear, a deep silence as he or she tells the story. It might be empathy or reassurance. It might be a hug as the mourner weeps, or respectful words of condolence. It might be companionship in grief, or a distracting story of one's day. It might be a remembrance of the one who is gone, or even a laugh over something they once said or did. I don't know how common it is to follow this etiquette, as I have never experienced shiva myself, but I do know that it makes perfect sense.

LEE BLUEMEL

Perhaps we try too hard to offer comfort in words. In many years of knowing, living with, people in time of grief, I have learned that the wounded spirit is sensitive to sustaining love in more and other things than words. The touch of a hand can dispel that terrible sense of aloneness. A silent presence, if it is that of a dear friend, can be more eloquent than the loveliest words. We may offer our tribute, but we do that for ourselves, not for the grief-stricken, for they know their loss as we cannot express it for them. It is something to know that others care. To know that other hands are reaching out through that seemingly impenetrable darkness which bears in upon the spirit, to know the tactile presence of love which respects our grief and shares it, keeping alight that little candle in our lives which flickered and seemed to go out as the darkness gathered us in, this is the service only love can offer, the service that can sustain.

ROBERT T. WESTON

Being with a person who has just lost someone to death is standing in a place of pain and mystery. It is a place where almost all words sound pale and silly. . . .

I'm not sure what to write to my friends who lost their son. But at least I'm not feeling like there's one perfect thing to say hovering just out of reach. My note will be inadequate. It will sound silly. Deep mysteries mock words. That's why we have poetry and sacred scriptures. We keep trying to figure out a way to speak to each other about life and God and love and death and other unfathomables. I'll keep trying, if you will.

MEG BARNHOUSE

When I Heard of Your Loss I Called

Your voice was like shattered crystal
on terrazzo
and I was barefoot
and walked across bleeding
reaching for you with my voice.

And we talked
of cabbages and kings
of why man's blood is boiling hot
and whether broken dreams have wings
and of the lives of galaxies
and turning tears to ink.

I could not speak then of healing
but I thought—
deeper than words I thought—
    Be well.

And slowly
your voice gathered itself together
as if invisible hands
touched rim to bowl to stem
and bid them hold.

PAT KING

Spirit of Life, we ask today for comfort. We are fearful creatures. It is hard to lose those we love. It is hard to lose our own lives, for this is all we know, all we have known. Let us live well today, for today is what we have been given. Let us live all our days with courage, that we may leave this world with hope. Let us rest in you, O Spirit of Life, knowing that we will never be forsaken. Amen.

MARILYN SEWELL

We aren't the giants we'd like so much to be, and the world can loom so large. When all is quiet and we are small and the night is dark, may we hear the tender breathing of all who lie awake with us in fear, that together we may gather strength to live with love, and kindness, and confidence.

JANE RZEPKA

O Mysterious God of Life and Death, Source of Love,
When our questions challenge a troubling and troubled world,
May courage remain with us.
When the mysteries—the pain of paradox and sorrow—knife us,
May deeper awareness and sensitivity guide us and enrich us.
May the Love of Truth comfort us and lead us.
May honesty of thought and deed unite in us, and thus
May the Spirit of Life renew us. Amen.

BRUCE SOUTHWORTH

Spirit of Life and Love,
moving in all things, in grasses and stars,
in waters and fields,
in every living thing,
and in each of us,
we are weeping.

We are frightened.
We are angry.
We are broken, seeking to be whole.
In our pain we wait for healing
(and we will find ways to heal each other).
In our confusion we wait for understanding
(though we know it may not come in our lifetimes).
In our loss, we wait for peace again, and a joyful and sustaining hope.
Spirit of life and love, moving through all things, we commend to
your embrace all those who mourn, all those who have died, and
our own lives.
Amen.

VICTORIA SAFFORD

The End Will Be Peace

The end of this life is what we call death—it is an hour in which words are spoken, things are seen and felt, that are kept in the secret chambers of the hearts of those who stand by, it is so that all of us have such things in our hearts or forebodings of such things. . . .

Much strive must be striven
Much suffering must be suffered
Much prayer must be prayed
And then the end will be peace.

VINCENT VAN GOGH

If we're very lucky, in tragedy we will tap into reserves we didn't know we had. I remember a woman whose husband died, leaving her to raise two young sons. Utterly devastated, she went to bed. As she tells it, she might never have gotten up, but she did get up, and there was really no mystery about it. One of the boys came into her room and said quite simply, "Mom, we're out of peanut butter." I think of the role model she provided for her children. Reeling from the blow, she determined to stagger to her feet again, and life went on.

KIM CRAWFORD HARVIE

All creation is precariously contained in a mended cup of meaning. It is the cup from which we drink our lives—the cup with which we drink to life. It is a cup that is broken and mended, broken and mended over and over again. Each time an era passes, a way of life is destroyed, or someone of significance to us dies, we cry out that our cup is broken, and so it is. Yet, somehow—together—we must find, we do find the way to mend it all over again.

Now we are faced with that task of meaning once more.

NICK CARDELL

Images of dry and thirsty lands and the importance of water are common in Hebrew and Christian Scriptures, and also in the less familiar writings of other religions which have sprung up in areas where rainfall is scarce. Stories of gatherings at wells are scattered through them; wells mark the places with names; water is the first hospitable gift to the stranger. And gradually we see dry times and places used to represent the hard times of both body and spirit. Water then becomes a symbol for those gifts and strengths that sustain us—that refresh the flow of life and love within us. A passage in Deuteronomy reminds us that we drink from wells we did not dig, enjoy other gifts that are not of our making. The Twenty-third Psalm speaks of still waters, of restoring the soul. The woman at the well gives Jesus a drink.

GRACE H. SIMONS

In the flowing of love, in the adoration of humility, there is no question of continuance.

RALPH WALDO EMERSON

Now there are some things we all know, but we don't take'm out and look at'm very often. We all know that *something* is eternal. And it ain't houses and it ain't names, and it ain't earth and it ain't even the stars . . . everybody knows in their bones that something is eternal, and that something has to do with human beings. All the greatest people who ever lived have been telling us that for five thousand years and yet you'd be surprised how people are always losing hold of it. There's something way down deep that's eternal about every human being.

THORNTON WILDER

Dear Lovely Death,
Change is thy other name.

LANGSTON HUGHES

Stars, Songs, Faces

Gather the stars if you wish it so.
Gather the songs and keep them.
Gather the faces of women.
Gather for keeping years and years.
And then . . .
Loosen your hands, let go and say good-by.
Let the stars and the songs go.
Let the faces and years go.
Loosen your hands and say good-by.

Carl Sandburg

Life as a whole never takes death seriously. It laughs, dances and plays, it builds, hoards and loves in death's face. Only when we detach one individual fact of death do we see its blankness and become dismayed. We lose sight of the wholeness of a life of which death is part. It is like looking at a piece of cloth through a microscope. It appears like a net; we gaze at the big holes and shiver in imagination. But the truth is, death is not the ultimate reality. It looks black, as the sky looks blue; but it does not blacken existence, just as the sky does not leave its stain upon the wings of the bird.

Rabindranath Tagore

The fabric of your life has been torn. It has been rent asunder, as they say. Now you must begin the reweaving of relationships so that the hole will be mended. You will see the broken place but the fabric will be made whole.

JEAN M. ROWE

When sorrow comes, let us accept it simply, as part of life. Let the heart be open to pain; let it be stretched by it. All the evidence we have says that this is the better way. An open heart never grows bitter. Or if it does, it cannot remain so. In the desolate hour, there is an outcry; a clenching of the hands upon emptiness; a burning pain of bereavement; a weary ache of loss. But anguish, like ecstasy, is not forever. There comes a gentleness, a returning quietness, a restoring stillness. This, too, is a door to life. Here, also, is a deepening of meaning—and it can lead to dedication; a going forward to the triumph of the soul, the conquering of the wilderness. And in the process will come a deepening inward knowledge that in the final reckoning, all is well.

A. POWELL DAVIES

Elegy for Thomas Haefemeyer

Who loses here:

the infant draped over his mother's arms
for the first time

or the family assembled behind,
alarmed at the sight of him

free of encumbrances,
free of the magicians

who kept him from them,
as from death,

reckoning his clockwork
could be changed?

A baby away from rooms this once
in the long light of afternoon:

an armful of lanterns
in an already luminous space,

paper-white above the shadows
and, after all, a gift.

JODY BOLZ

In our times of suffering, may we find the courage to look into the experience of our pain. When it passes, as it surely will, may we find a true pearl, true grace, or a graceful flower growing out of the muck, decay, and mud. May we find that we emerge from these experiences more whole, more free, more open to beauty, truth, and grace. May we find that we are stronger in the broken places of our lives.

DEBORAH CAYER

The work of grieving is a journey back to new life. The wound may be deep; it does not go away. Rather, the wound too becomes part of the new life; it gives us a new way of being ourselves. We become life going on after loss and grief, life going on to new experiences and joys, life going on to greater compassion and wisdom. These are hard-won gains, but they are ours and they make us who we are. For that reason we celebrate and give thanks for the dead, who have given us new life.

JUDITH E. MEYER

We are not meant to stay wounded. We are supposed to move through our tragedies and challenges and to help each other move through the many painful episodes of our lives. By remaining stuck in the power of our wounds, we block our own transformation. We overlook the greater gifts inherent in our wounds—the strength to overcome them and the lessons that we are meant to receive through them. Wounds are the means through which we enter the hearts of other people. They are meant to teach us to become compassionate and wise.

CAROLINE MYSS

Learning the Twenty-third Psalm by heart has proved helpful on more than one occasion when I've been with a family at the moment their loved one died. Even when a death is expected, even when it is the end of pain and suffering, there is a moment of shock and surprise when the loved one's breathing stops. Then those words, "Yea, though I walk through the valley of the shadow of death I will fear no evil for Thou art with me," become a lifeline to reality.

These mourners do not believe in a God who is a literal cosmic shepherd with a rod and staff. They do not believe that they shall not want. On the contrary, they know all too well that they will want their loved one back for the rest of their lives. They do not believe that they will leave the memorial service to lie down in green pastures or beside still waters. They know they will lie down, that night and for many to come, with a box of tissues and their hearts aching, minds racing, and stomachs churning. In short, the people I've known who ask for the Twenty-third Psalm to be incorporated in the memorial service do so not because they literally believe these words. They do so because, as countless generations have discovered, these words have the power to inspire, comfort, and strengthen in spiritually difficult times.

We need not live in fear that we are isolated beings in a random and careless universe. We need not live in fear of failure or not having or being enough. We need not live in fear that the demands of life will deplete us. We need not live in fear of death, our own or that of loved ones. We need not live in fear of enemies or foes. We need not live in fear that our lives do not have meaning and purpose. We need not live in fear.

Whether we call it the Lord or Mother, my Shepherd, or the Holy of Holies, or simply the Good within, we can trust that in this universe we will be cared for somehow, cradled in the embrace of a life larger than our own, healed and restored to wholeness in spite of whatever ails us, in spite of whatever is broken in our lives and world. In times of fear, grief, or doubt, there is a presence that will not forsake us. That is the promise made in the first line of the Twenty-third Psalm.

CLARE L. PETERSBERGER

The Lord is my shepherd; I shall not want.

He maketh me to lie down in green pastures: he leadeth me beside the still waters.

He restoreth my soul: he leadeth me in the paths of righteousness for his name's sake. Yea, though I walk through the valley of the shadow of death, I will fear no evil: for thou art with me; thy rod and thy staff they comfort me.

Thou preparest a table before me in the presence of mine enemies: thou anointest my head with oil; my cup runneth over.

Surely goodness and mercy shall follow me all the days of my life: and I will dwell in the house of the Lord for ever.

PSALM 23

This Many-Splendored Thing

I look to mother Earth with a cry upon my lips, "What is your answer to the age-old question, if a person dies, shall that person live again?"

And the earth was silent. Only a robin sang from the treetop
and a crocus pushed its way through the leaves,
lifting its face to the sun.

I gazed at the skies arching over my mead, "O Ye universes beyond universes, flying galaxies and stupendous distances, what hint have you of humankind's destiny beyond the rim of time?"

Silence from the darkening heavens. Only a whisper from those far off worlds telling of wonders lying only as a dream in the human heart.

I stood tip-toe to Life and flung my question down eons of time, "What is this many-splendored thing within our minds, coursing through our veins, flooding our souls and lifting our faces to the stars,—this Something that cannot die?"

No answer came from out the vast tomb of the years; but the spring flushed green across the ancient hills and Something in the heart of spring stirred that can never die.

I saw the evil and injustice under the sun, and heard the bitter cries of human pain; the sad farewells at the time of parting, and the universal query on the lips.

No answer came, but the surge of Life went through the earth and filled the skies; eternal life and love which conquer death. Life—endless, triumphant!

ALFRED S. COLE

Alchemy

I lift my heart as spring lifts up
A yellow daisy to the rain;
My heart will be a lovely cup
Altho' it holds but pain.
For I shall learn from flower and leaf
That color every drop they hold,
To change the lifeless wine of grief
To living gold.

SARA TEASDALE

Autumn's story does not promise an end to suffering and mourning and tears. Autumn's story does not promise eternity to any particular soul. It does not claim that we will achieve perfection. Rather, Autumn's claim is that our lives progress through cycles, that the full measure of our humanity includes our death. Autumn's promise is that we have available to us the possibility of wholeness in this life, but our wholeness includes our dying. Autumn challenges us not to give ourselves over to visions of eternity sketched out in ancient texts but to align ourselves with the spirit of life, which flows within and among us and carries us ultimately to our physical end. As leaves fall in November wind, Autumn's story is one of imperfection: "You will mourn; you will make mistakes; you will grieve; you will cause pain and you will feel pain; you will die. But that same wind that buffets leaves as they descend from branch to earth says as well that the Spirit of Life is with us through it all, available to us as a guide, a source of strength and solace." To align ourselves with the falling leaves, to open ourselves up to the sadness that accompanies our living and our dying, is not to surrender to something beyond our control. Rather, it is a movement of reconciliation with Nature's way and the Spirit of Life.

JOSHUA MASON PAWELEK

I used to think that cemeteries had to go—prideful luxury and waste of space I called them. Today I eat those words.

Cemeteries in greater Boston make up 35 percent of the open space remaining in the area, and how that space is used! Two men studied this space last year and encountered 95 species of birds, including beyond robins, blue jays and starlings, the yellow-shafted flickers, ring-necked pheasants, mockingbirds, bobwhites, black-billed cuckoos, belted kingfishers, Wilson's warblers, rufous-sided towhees, and great blue herons.

It finally has dawned on me that these creatures have as much right to the sky as the high rises. And who is humankind to crowd out other inhabitants of "land-consuming" graveyards? Our investigators found in our greater Boston burial grounds the homes of raccoons, striped skunks, red foxes, woodchucks, flying squirrels, red squirrels, opossums, muskrats, cottontails. Not to mention garter snakes, turtles, newts, salamanders, toads, bullfrogs, a variety of fish and other proliferations of God's creativity.

It turns out that what was once necropolis becomes the guarantor of life, a center of vitalism, an oasis of ecological sanity. The receptacle of death becomes the fountain of being—a home for birds and beasts and trees, and according to our investigators, a place of jogging, Frisbee, hide-and-seek, hopscotch, card playing, berry picking, model plane flying, lunch eating, dog walking, relaxing and sleeping, and coming to terms with family and history by graveside visitation. Also, Marvell notwithstanding, the grave's a fine and pleasant place and many there do embrace.

It's not easy to change your mind—but let's hear it: Viva graveyards! Viva the larger wisdom that confounds our own!"

CLARKE DEWEY WELLS

When the Bottom Falls Out

Sometimes, when the bottom falls out of life, we are set free. We attain enlightenment, or an enlightenment of sorts; some perspective, some clarity, some sense of reality, some sense of dealing with things as they are, some relief from anxiety and perplexity because something profound has happened.

Whenever that profound thing happens, we can expect to go through a process, sometimes a long process, a painful or at least uncomfortable process, in which we let go of something and slowly learn how to live again. This is true no matter what we love: a loved one, a work, a hope, a vision, an image of ourselves, a part of ourselves. Loss makes artist of us all as we weave new patterns in the fabric of our lives.

GRETA W. CROSBY

The death of a dear friend, wife, brother, lover, which seemed nothing but privation, somewhat later assumes the aspect of a guide or genius; for it is commonly operates revolutions in our way of life, terminates an epoch of infancy or of youth which was waiting to be closed, breaks up a wonted occupation, or a household, or style of living, and allows the formation of new ones more friendly to the growth of character.

RALPH WALDO EMERSON

We don't ignore the harsh realities of life, the very real causes for despair that come now and again into our lives and all lives.

We recognize them.

We weep and lament in our anger and our grief.

We strive together to find meaning or simply ways to keep going when pain or death or hatred or injustice or the apparent randomness of life strike at our very souls, and despair seems the only possible response.

And then, in the midst of it all, we celebrate life, the life that goes on in and among and through all the causes for despair. For as long as there is life, there is hope. And where there is living hope, tended and protected by a loving community, despair cannot triumph.

LISA DOEGE

This is the greatest skill of all,
to take the bitter with the sweet and make it beautiful,
to take the whole of life in all its moods,
its strengths and weaknesses,
and of the whole make one great and celestial harmony.

ROBERT T. WESTON

Inescapably in the course of our lives we must each sometime face the contradictions which threaten to undermine all sense of purpose or meaning. . . . It is when our spirits face such chasms of emptiness that we can begin to understand the meaning of despair. For we have seen destruction in a thousand forms. Yet never in our experience has destruction been so complete that there was nothing to survive. In the stream of time this may not always continue to be true. But the spirit finds a parable in the survivals we have seen: something there is, which is eternal. Something there is, about ourselves, about our living, about the things which are precious, which has a setting in more than just this minute. Something there is which, no matter what occurs in nature or history, is ineradicable. In this faith in the life-renewing way, in that which does not perish, we too may find a ground to stand upon. Nothing can take away the beauty and significance of life.

WALTER ROYAL JONES

They who stand with breaking hearts around this little grave need have no fear. The larger and the nobler faith in all that is and is to be, tells us that death, even at its worst, is only perfect rest. We know that through the common wants of life, the needs and duties of each hour, their grief will lessen day by day, until at last these graves will be to them a place of rest and peace, almost of joy. There is for them this consolation, the dead do not suffer. If they live again, their lives will surely be as good as ours. We have no fear; we are all the children of the same mother, and the same fate awaits us all. We, too, have our religion, and it is this: "Help for the living; hope for the dead."

ROBERT INGERSOLL

A tomb is no place to stay
When each morning announces our reprieve,
And we know we are granted yet another day of living.

RICHARD S. GILBERT

Let our lives be about thank you. Let our lives be about praise. Praise everything. The beauty of this mutilated world. The joy of eye and ear and touch and scent.

Why? Because it is so much better than lament. It is so much more useful than despair. Hopelessness leaves us with no possibilities and no options. Lament is necessary, but we must not get stuck there. Despair is the end of the road.

BETH MILLER

This is the joy to all forever free: life springs from death and shatters every fetter, And winter turns to spring eternally.

ROBERT T. WESTON

We have great depths within us that we have never plumbed, great insight and intuition, great reservoirs of love. The path to them leads through places of emptiness and fear. Let us pray for courage and perseverance as we seek the treasure of our own hidden places. May we learn the wisdom of letting go.

DANIEL DENNIS

Let us celebrate the power of memory to give us hope.
Let us pray for the power of memory to help us heal.
Let us honor the many gifts we were given by our beloved.
Our challenge is to affirm and celebrate the joy, goodness, and
    beauty of life.

LONE I. JENSEN

We, too, will be blessed by the spring.
We will once again notice the
love and compassion that come to us each day.
We will fill our hearts with the
comfort and cheer that make our lives glad.
We will be open to the new opportunities
and adventures that unexpectedly come our way.
Once again we will love, and believe, and laugh,
And hope, and give, and wonder, and rejoice.
May we be forever grateful
that we have been so richly blessed by the gift of life.
May we give thanks for the rich complexity of our lives.
May we know that although winter is upon us,
it will give way to spring, and then summer,
and fall and then to winter, once again.
May we sing praises for all the seasons of the year
and for all the seasons of our lives.
Amen.

SYLVIA L'HERROU HOWE

Song

When I am dead, my dearest,
Sing no sad songs for me;
Plant thou no roses at my head,
Nor shady cypress tree:
Be the green grass above me
With showers and dewdrops wet;
And if thou wilt, remember,
And if thou wilt, forget.
I shall not see the shadows,
I shall not feel the rain;
I shall not hear the nightingale
Sing on, as if in pain;
And dreaming through the twilight
That doth not rise nor set,
Haply I may remember,
And haply may forget.

Christina Rossetti

If I should go before the rest of you
Break not a flower or inscribe a stone,
Nor when I'm gone speak in a Sunday voice
But be the usual selves that I have known.

Weep if you must,
Parting is hell,
But life goes on,
So sing as well.

JOYCE GRENFELL

The Great Peace

Always there is something,
Something that lives on when folly has burned itself out;
When the leaves are sere; and fall, one by one;
When the hair is white,
And the hands tremble,
And cannot quite find what they seek;
Always there is something.
Perhaps it is a whisper in the night,
Or a great silence, when the planes are gone,
And the cars are silent beside the highways,
And the children are asleep,
And the heart can hear a soundless voice.
Always there is something, something beyond all time.
The past that has hurt slips away;
The humiliations, the failures, the resentment,

The sorrows, the haunting fears, dissolve into the healing night.
The darkness is no longer darkness, but a comforting presence,
And it comes, a great peace, flooding the heart.
It comes, a sense of healing forgiveness,
A sense of comprehending and forgiving compassion,
A meaning in which all things are comprehended and made whole
Though we, accepting, comprehend it not.
Always there is something and we, knowing this, need never fear
    again,
Nor hate, nor grieve, for there is always something
Above defeat and success alike,
And to know and feel this
Is to know the great peace.

ROBERT T. WESTON

Our voices may be the voices of grief, but the language after which grief gropes is the language of Love. And we . . . come in Love's name to express, for those whose lies have not had the visible presence of Love, a calm and abiding trust in Love's immortality and consecrating power.

ROBERT T. WESTON

You must not grieve for me.
Death does not change our love for one another:
That love still lives on; it does not lessen,
Always I am yours, and you are mine.
Sometimes the heart asks more than life can give,
But Peace will come, and it will make us wise.

HAZEL ROGERS GREDLER

Love Abides

Often we are found in our grief and comforted
    calmed by some kindness
      brought alive again by beauty
      that catches us undefended.

Even when the sun is most thin and far
even at the hour the storm is at its height
we can go through
    renewal nests within sorrow
      love abides, even beyond anger, beyond death.

We are held in an embrace invisible but infinite
moving with all creation

between wholeness and fragmentation
moving always toward the one.

Small joys and great sorrows pass
and we, with steps uncertain, move on
to whatever is next

but continually seen, heard, held
by Life infinite and remote, intimate and abiding.

Love, do not let us go.   Amen.

BARBARA PESCAN

But soon we shall die and all memory of those five will have left the
earth, and we ourselves shall be loved for a while and forgotten. But
the love will have been enough; all those impulses of love return to
the love that made them. Even memory is not necessary for love.
There is a land of the living and a land of the dead and the bridge is
love, the only survival, the only meaning.

THORNTON WILDER

The Right to Die

I have no fancy for that ancient cant
That makes us masters of our destinies,
And not our lives, to hold or give them up
As will directs; I cannot, will not think
That men, the subtle worms, who plot and plan
And scheme and calculate with such shrewd wit,
Are such great blund'ring fools as not to know
When they have lived enough.

    Men court not death
When there are sweets still left in life to taste.
Nor will a brave man choose to live when he,
Full deeply drunk of life, has reached the dregs,
And knows that now but bitterness remains.
He is the coward who, outfaced in this,
Fears the false goblins of another life.
I honor him who being much harassed
Drinks of sweet courage until drunk of it,—
Then seizing Death, reluctant, by the hand,
Leaps with him, fearless, to eternal peace!

PAUL LAURENCE DUNBAR

How shall we face the death of those whom we love? With that very love in our hearts. With tears in our eyes. With thanks for the gift of their having been part of our lives and we a part of theirs. With a recognition that though the pain of loss is real and powerful and more than a little frightening, the love that binds us all together is yet stronger, yet more real, and enormously comforting. I really do believe that death comes to the body but never to the loving heart.

KENNETH W. COLLIER

No, we do not forgive and forget. But when we invite the power of forgiveness, we release ourselves from some of the destructive hold the past has on us. Our hatred, our anger, our need to feel wronged—those will destroy us, whether a relationship is reconciled or not.

But we cannot just will ourselves to enter into forgiveness, either as givers or receivers. We can know it is right and that we want to do it and still not be able to.

We can, however, be open and receptive to the power of forgiveness, which, like any gift of the spirit, isn't of our own making. Its power is rooted in love. The Greek word for this kind of love is *agape*. Martin Luther King, Jr., defined *agape* as "Love seeking to preserve and create community." This kind of love is human, but it is also the grace of a transcendent power that lifts us out of ourselves. It transforms and heals; and even when we are separated by time or space or death, it reconciles us to ourselves and to Life. For its power abides not just between us but within us. If we invited the power of *agape* to heal our personal wounds and give us the gift of forgiveness, we would give our world a better chance of survival.

SARAH YORK

The clouds that gather round the setting sun
Do take a sober colouring from an eye
That hath kept a watch o'er man's mortality;
Another race hath been, and other palms are won.
Thanks to the human heart by which we live,
Thanks to its tenderness, its joys and fears,
To me the meanest flower that blows can give
Thoughts that do often lie too deep for tears.

WILLIAM WORDSWORTH

To Fill the Void

I do not care if your true god controls
the whole sweet universe or just your own
small piece of it. Your god may fit black holes
and worms in some grand scheme and rule alone
or with a multitude of jealous gods

or spirits of wild animals and trees.
This god may want you sacrificed, or awed
by sacred myths, or praying on your knees.
That god may let you meditate or smoke
cigars and twirl around. You may prefer
a god or goddess, think it's all a joke—
there is no god, just science, cold and pure.
Just tell me you belong, your faith's enough
to let you sleep at night, despite sure death.

MARY ZOLL

She Speaks of Death

Oblivion, she said
in a weary voice,
is what is after death.
    There is nothing after death
    but nothing
    and that's all right with me.

It made good scientific sense,
nailed to the cathedral door
of her religious childhood.

And when her husband died
a few years later
oblivion
pinned against eternity
sagged in the middle
and it its folds
sweet disbelief surprised her
and the hope
she hadn't seen the last of him yet.

BARBARA PESCAN

Oneness

The moment I die
I will try to come back to you
as quickly as possible.
I promise it will not take long.
Isn't it true
I am already with you,
as I die each moment?
I come back to you
in every moment.
Just look,
feel my presence.

If you want to cry,
please cry.
And know
that I will cry with you.
The tears you shed
will heal us both.
Your tears are mine.
The earth I tread this morning
transcends history.
Spring and Winter are both present in the moment.
The young leaf and the dead leaf are really one.
My feet touch deathlessness,
and my feet are yours.
Walk with me now.
Let us enter the dimension of oneness
and see the cherry tree blossom in Winter.
Why should we talk about death?
I don't need to die
to be back with you.

THICH NHAT HANH

What though the radiance which was once so bright
Be now for ever taken from my sight,

Though nothing can bring back the hour
Of splendour in the grass, of glory in the flower;
We will grieve not, rather find
Strength in what remains behind;
In the primal sympathy
Which having been must ever be;
In the soothing thoughts that spring
Out of human suffering;
In the faith that looks through death,
In years that bring the philosophic mind.

WILLIAM WORDSWORTH

O Spirit of Life,
We have gathered this day to acknowledge your presence within
every moment, every detail of our daily lives. Slowly we men and
women and children come to recognize our vulnerability—to pain,
to illness, to failure, to loss, and finally to death. Somehow, slowly,
we must come to terms with these realities. At times, we are in
danger of succumbing to despair.

Embrace us here, lifting us out of discouragement, connecting us
with one another and with the energy and hope that dwell all around
and within us. Help us, not to forget our griefs, but to accept them
as part of life—so that we may face them, and weep, and then turn
our faces to the future. Help us remember the strength and the

courage and the beauty of the loved ones we have lost, so that their lives are carried on in our lives. Help us to reach out to one another, not to cling but to understand and feel the love and the wisdom of our earthly companions. Help us to see, ever more clearly, the immeasurable goodness and preciousness of life itself.

So may we open our heart in this time of quiet meditation, finding peace and hope.

Amen.

HELEN L. COHEN

If we can say that grace is a sense of connectedness, that it is the experience of our underlying nature, then we may see how what is often called tragedy holds the seeds of grace. We see that what brings us to grace is not always pleasant, though it seems always to take us to something essential in ourselves.

STEPHEN LEVINE

Having a disability has one good effect. I am far more aware of and sympathetic about the illnesses some of my friends are struggling to surmount than I was when I was well. It is companionable to share some of the day-to-day triumphs and despairs. I'm afraid terribly cheerful, well people are no help at all!

I am aware for the first time perhaps what courage it takes to grow old, how exasperating it is no longer to be able to do what seemed nothing at all even a year ago.

MAY SARTON

We trust that beyond the absence:
there is a presence.

That beyond the pain:
there can be healing.

That beyond the brokenness:
there can be wholeness.

That beyond the hurting:
there may be forgiveness.

That beyond the silence:
there may be the word.

That beyond the word:
there may be understanding.

That through all understanding:
there is love.

ANONYMOUS

Life Again

Out of the dusk a shadow,
Then, a spark.

Out of the cloud a silence,
Then, a lark.

Out of the heart a rapture,
Then, a pain.

Out of the dead, cold ashes,
Life again.

JOHN BANISTER TABB

A vision of the larger hope sees the essential goodness of existence despite the specifics of any given moment. Events happen, but to isolate bad times and then turn them into personal attacks is no more appropriate than to isolate good times and turn them into evidence of personal divine favor. The larger hope is about an overall pattern in which the many events of life play out, no one point in the pattern defining the whole, unless we choose to dwell and focus on it as if it were.

There is meaning in the pattern.

We can see the possibilities wherever we are in life, even on the other side of the worst tragedies we can imagine.

RANDOLPH W. B. BECKER

I stretch lame hands of faith, and grope,
    And gather dust and chaff, and call
    To what I feel is Lord of all,
And faintly trust the larger hope.

ALFRED LORD TENNYSON

Notes from the Other Side

I divested myself of despair
and fear when I came here.

Now there is no more catching
one's own eye in the mirror,

there are no bad books, no plastic,
no insurance premiums, and of course
no illness. Contrition
does not exist, nor gnashing

of teeth. No one howls as the first
clod of earth hits the casket.

The poor we no longer have with us.
Our calm hearts strike only the hour,

and God, as promised, proves
to be mercy clothed in light.

JANE KENYON

The colors of bright autumn and the bright sun
Tell of the beauty of that which dies
But always comes again.
They speak directly to the heart
Of the eternal which outlives all moments
And yet lives only in them,
Outlives all forms, yet comes again in them as in ourselves. . . .

There is a sadness in the autumn leaf:
I feel a sorrow that its beauty dies
And feel its message for the lives of those,
As of myself, whom I have known and loved.
The leaf comes not again, though other leaves

And flowers will bloom and other lives,
Richer that we have been, shall take our place.
Perhaps the autumn teaches us a wiser grace
Through which we live, by learning to let go.

ROBERT T. WESTON

The Trees

The trees are coming into leaf
Like something almost being said;
The recent buds relax and spread,
Their greenness is a kind of grief.

Is it they are born again
And we grow old? No, they die too.
Their yearly trick of looking new
Is written down in rings of grain.
Yet still the unresting catles thresh
In fullgrown thickness every May.
Last year is dead, they seem to say,
Begin afresh, afresh, afresh.

PHILIP LARKIN

Nature

As a fond mother, when the day is o'er,
    Leads by the hand her little child to bed,
    Half willing, half reluctant to be led,
    And leave his broken playthings on the floor,
Still gazing at them through the open door,
    Nor wholly reassured and comforted
    By promises of others in their stead,
    Which though more splendid, may not please him more;
So Nature deals with us, and takes away
    Our playthings one by one, and by the hand
    Leads us to rest so gently, that we go
Scarce knowing if we wish to go or stay,
Being too full of sleep to understand
How far the unknown transcends the what we know.

HENRY WADSWORTH LONGFELLOW

159

They Are Not Gone

They are not gone who pass
Beyond the clasp of hand,
Out from the strong embrace.
They are but come so close
We need not grope with hands,
Nor look to see, nor try
To catch the sound of feet.
They have put off their shoes
Softly to walk by day
Within our thoughts, to tread
At night our dream-led paths
Of sleep.

HUGH ROBERT ORR

We can take time to remember those who have gone before us, to name them and identify their presence in the things around us—in checkerboards and cedar chests, the curve of a cheekbone and the turn of a phrase, in spaghetti sauce and old sweaters. By spending time and paying attention, we allow things that are already there to speak to us. We can hear the voices of our ancestors in the crackling of a hearth fire or the rush of a wave upon a shore.

ANNA RUSSOMANO BROSKIE

I was helping my five-year old daughter, Sidney, brush her teeth one morning when she informed me that after I died, she would talk to me in heaven. Given my perfect state of health, I was startled by this unexpected turn in our conversation.

After I regained my composure, I said, "So you think I'll be going up to heaven after I die, somewhere up in the sky?" Without a moment's hesitation, she answered, "No, not somewhere up in the sky. Heaven is everywhere. Like God. When you're in heaven, you'll be with me everywhere."

I found this a rather lovely idea. Instead of imagining heaven as a special, other place, Sidney construed heaven existentially—in terms of an everlasting presence in this place.

"Do you remember how I told you my Daddy died?" I asked. "Well, sometimes I feel like he's very near me. Sometimes I even think I can talk to him."

Sidney nodded gravely. And then she explained, "That's the reason people pray."

I repeated what I'd understood her to say: "You mean, people pray so they can talk to the people they loved who have died?"

She smiled yes.

MYRIAM RENAUD WITH SIDNEY RENAUD-EBERLY

Hear in the wind
The bushes sobbing,
It is the sigh of our forefathers.

BIRAGO DIOP

At age eight, my granddaughter, Laura, was at a critical age—old enough to be curious about lots of things, yet young enough to still profit from the experience of adults. So it seemed the perfect time to introduce her to the world of her grandfather as a child—a rural world far from the city life she sees daily. Our trip included a visit to the one-room schoolhouse I attended and the house in which I was born (Laura wondered aloud if it might be a log cabin). For my own benefit, we visited a remote Missouri cemetery where family members going back to my great-great-grandfather and many of his descendants are buried.

To my delight, Laura was intrigued by the concept of so much family history within the small confines of the cemetery, as well as her own ties to pioneer settlers in early nineteenth-century Missouri. The fact that my great-grandfather bore the name Jefferson Davis Mason only added to the intrigue. As we walked around the cemetery, she raced from headstone to headstone, gathering genealogical information and carefully noting the complex relationships wrought by the early deaths and multiple marriages of rural life more than a century ago. She noted with interest the several family members who had died in infancy so long ago.

Children, it seems to me, cope with death better than adults do. By the time they are in elementary school, most have experienced the death of a pet or at least understand the concept of death as it applies to insects and wildlife. Taking children to a family cemetery can bring to life, through death, a family history that is difficult to relate in abstract terms. I recommend it.

DENNIS E. MASON AND LAURA NOLAN

Even the death of Friends will inspire us as much as their lives. They will leave consolation to the mourners, as the rich leave money to defray the expenses of their funerals, and their memories will be incrusted over with sublime and pleasing thoughts, as monuments of other men are overgrown with moss; for our Friends have no place in the graveyard.

HENRY DAVID THOREAU

They say: We leave you our
deaths. Give them their meaning.

ARCHIBALD MACLEISH

I am loath to close. We are not enemies, but friends. We must not be
enemies. Though passion may have strained, it must not break our
bonds of affection. The mystic chords of memory, stretching from
every battle-field, and patriot grave, to every living heart and hearth-
stone, all over this broad land, will yet swell the chorus of the Union,
when again touched, as surely they will be, by the better angels of our
nature.

ABRAHAM LINCOLN

The dead are truly dead, yet as they truly live on in us, as we will
    live on in our successors, as long as the earth is disturbed and
    blessed by living creatures riding on its broad back.
As we say good-bye to them, we bid them welcome again to our
    minds and our hearts.

KENNETH PATTON

The greatest name will perish from human history, the finest monument crumble into dust, and the time will come when our names will be lost and our places know us no more. Yet we shall survive in the memories of our friends as long as the remembrance will serve any good purpose, and then our work and thought and influence will mingle with the great ocean of human achievement, and the sum total of that will be something more, and something different from what it would have been without us.

AUGUSTA CHAPIN

Living, you made it goodlier to live,
Dead, you will make it easier to die.

GEORGE SANTAYANA

Nobody replaces anybody.
People are simply irreplaceable.
Those who touch our lives with meaning
remain with us forever,
for good and for ill.
People come and go,
passing through our lives,

leaving an indelible mark on us.
Other people come and go,
leaving us enriched and devastated.
They do not replace anybody.
The build and sustain the community.

DAVID E. BUMBAUGH

Death This Year

Death this year has taken men
Whose kind we shall not see again.
Pride and skill and friendliness,
Wrath and wisdom and delight,
Are shining still, but shining less,
And clouded to the common sight.
Time will show them clear again.
Time will give us other men
With names to write in burning gold
When they are great and we are old,
But these were royal-hearted, rare
Memory keeps with loving care
Deeds they did and tales they told.
But living men are hard to spare.

JOHN HOLMES

To see things under the form of eternity is to see them in their historic and moral truth, not as they seemed when they passed, but as they remain when they are over. When a man's life is over, it remains true that he has lived; it remains true that he has been one sort of man, and not another. In the infinite mosaic of history that bit has its unfading colour and its perpetual function and effect.

A man who understands himself under the form of eternity knows the quality that eternally belongs to him, and knows that he cannot wholly die, even if he would; for when the movement of his life is over, the truth of his life remains. The fact of him is a part forever of the infinite context of facts.

GEORGE SANTAYANA

What is it that you need to do, in the face of death, to make your life shine in the memory of others and to die with a satisfied mind, as the old song says? It's probably going to be a different answer for each of you, but there's consensus in the great religions of the world that it has something to do with loving and serving and letting go of our greed, our ignorance, and our hatred. Let it be about awakening to the present moment, when the infinite beauty of the universe is available to you with all its joy and pain.

ARVID STRAUBE

Mysterious death! who in a single hour
    Life's gold can so refine,
    And by thy art divine
Bending beneath the weight of eighty years,
    Spent with the noble strife
    Of a victorious life,
We watched her fading heavenward, through our tears.

But ere the sense of loss our hearts had wrung,
    A miracle was wrought,
    And swift as happy thought
She lived again, brave, beautiful, and young.

Age, Pain, and Sorrow dropped the veils they wore,
    And showed the tender eyes
    Of angels in disguise,
Whose discipline so patiently she bore.

The past years brought their harvest rich and fair,
    While Memory and Love
    Together fondly wove
A golden garland for the silver hair.

How could we mourn like those who are bereft,
    When every pang of grief

found balm for its relief
In counting up the treasures she had left?

Faith that withstood the shocks of toil and time,
        Hope that defied despair,
        Patience that conquered care,
And loyalty, whose courage was sublime. . . .

We thought to weep, but sing for joy instead,
        Full of the grateful peace
        That followed her release;
For nothing but the weary dust lies dead.

LOUISA MAY ALCOTT

Kings and queens we are, in memory and in the love that exists among the living, and which is woven between us and those who dwell among us only in spirit. In this hour we weave the strands ever more closely together and call into our circle of faith our friends and loved ones of blessed memory.

VICTORIA WEINSTEIN

They Are With Us Still

In the struggles we choose for ourselves, in the ways we move forward in our lives and bring our world forward with us, it is right to remember the names of those who gave us strength in this choice of living. It is right to name the power of hard lives well-lived. We share a history with those lives. We belong to the same motion. They too were strengthened by what had gone before. They too were drawn on by the vision of what might come to be.

Those who lived before us, who struggled for justice and suffered injustice before us, have not melted into the dust, and have not disappeared. They are with us still. The lives they lived hold us steady. Their words remind us and call us back to ourselves. Their courage and love evoke our own.

We, the living, carry them with us: we are their voices, their hands and their hearts. We take them with us, and with them choose the deeper path of living.

KATHLEEN MCTIGUE

Born of the sun they traveled a short while towards the sun and left the vivid air signed with their honor.

STEPHEN SPENDER

On this day,
let us pause to remember those who have come before us,
those who have helped to bring us to where we are today—
members of our families,
members of this community,
friends and neighbors,
leaders of women and men.
And on this day,
let us have a special silence for those whose names are lost to us,
and lost to history,
but whose efforts, large and small, have mattered—
in ways we will never know.

Today,
as we look toward the future,
we give thanks for the past,
and the legacy we are blessed to continue.
May we live our lives so that they have mattered,
in large ways and in small,
in ways we may never know.

KATHRYN A. SCHMITZ

Her finely touched spirit had still its fine issues, though they were not widely visible. Her full nature, like that river of which Cyrus broke the strength, spent itself in channels which had no great name on the earth. But the effect of her being on those around her was incalculably diffusive: for the growing good of the world is partly dependent on unhistoric acts; and that things are not so ill with you and me as they might have been, is half owing to the number who lived faithfully a hidden life, and rest in unvisited tombs.

George Eliot

The very best thing we can do, both in grieving and in supporting others in their grief, is to articulate the ways in which the one who has been lost to us will be carried forward in our lives. This is the great challenge of life in the face of loss: Can we make of our lives altars to our dead, and so, through our lives, give them life?

Who lives on in you? In small part, when I am patient, funny, or generous; when I tell stories or talk about the weather; when I am kind, especially to children and elders; when I love without condition, my grandfather lives on in me, and among us, and my grief gives way to joy. So may it be for us all: May our grief give way to joy.

Kim Crawford Harvie

It is the time of the year,
it is the time to cast away your fear,
and enter deep within the Earth
where spirits play the bones for birth.

Laughing, we dance together,
holding hands with Death.
Weeping, we greet our loved ones
who from earthly planes have left.

Weaving the circle
with garlands of love,
binding all life
from below and above.
Sing out their names now!
Give their memory breath!

MARYLYN MOTHERBEAR SCOTT

I cannot think of them as dead who walk with me no more; along
the path of life I tread they are but gone before . . .

And still their silent ministry within my heart has place as when
on earth they walked with me and met me face to face.

FREDERICK HOSMER

Memory

My memory is a haunted house;
    in all the empty rooms are ghosts benign.

In loneliness I'm never quite alone;
    my houses o'er run with those no longer here.

In work-filled hours and in the dark of night
    I hear again the voices long since stilled.

Friends sit before my fire in lively talk,
    and at my table gather they that were.

Across the floors go children's scuffling feet,
    withal, a never-fading presence waits.

Sometimes ill-meaning sprites knock at the gates
    to disinter old follies and mistakes.

They have their way, for in a haunted house
    there is no keeping out, or keeping in.

CLINTON LEE SCOTT

When I die
Give what's left of me away
To children
And old men that wait to die.
And if you need to cry,
Cry for your brother
Walking the street beside you.
And when you need me,
Put your arms around anyone
And give them
What you need to give to me.

I want to leave you something,
Something better
Than words
Or sounds.

Look for me
In the people you've known
Or loved,
And if you cannot give me away
At least let me live on your eyes
And not on your mind.

You can love me most
By letting

Hands touch hands,
By letting
Bodies touch bodies,
And by letting go
Of children
That need to be free.

Love doesn't die,
People do.
So, when all that's left of me
Is love,
Give me away.

MERRITT MALLOY

One of time's greatest boons is its softening of the angularities of pain. Sorrow's wounds heal, though not without scar. Grief's sharp jabbing thrusts or its aching emptiness give way to peace and sanctifying memory. That which has been, and is no more, remains within the mind to bless. The anguish is drained away. Remembering, we discover the meaning of the beatitude: "Blessed are they that mourn, for they shall be comforted." "To suffer passes away," say the French, "but to have suffered never passes."

According to an ancient legend, a woman came to the river Styx to be ferried to the land of the departed spirits. Charon, the ferryman, reminded her of her privilege to drink of the waters of Lethe, which would allow her to forget the life she was leaving. "I will forget how I have suffered," she exclaimed. "Yes," replied Charon, "and also how you have rejoiced." "I will forget how I have been hated." "And also," said the ferryman, "how you have been loved." After thinking it over, the woman left the draught of Lethe untasted. Better the mingled memories of suffering and sorrow, joy and love, than oblivion.

ARTHUR FOOTE

His influence is a silent legend passed from generation to generation, told in lives, if not in words, spoken in smile and kindnesses, in wordless courage.

He lives in the way the people walk, in the course of their thought, in the pride that begets humility, in the criticism of self that begets mercy to others.

The generations forget his words; they remember the attitude and spirit of his person.

KENNETH PATTON

Memory

I taught once at a farm school in Vermont, where it was the custom on Memorial Day to visit all the little cemeteries in the countryside nearby. There were many of these—some in churchyards or next to open fields where churches used to be, some on windy hillsides, some hidden far back in the woods, overgrown with brush and brambles, dimly defined in the shadows by the remnants of a low stone wall. These expeditions were led by the teacher at the school, a native of the town who remembered where all these forgotten places were. Children and teachers together piled into several cars and went to maybe six or seven graveyards in a day. At the entrance to each one, the teacher had us join hands in two rows of ten or twelve and then slowly walk the grounds, looking out for graves of veterans, many marked by little metal signposts but some so old we had to bend and squint and read the wind-smooth stones. They dated to the Revolutionary War and the War of 1812, the Civil War, the two world wars, and the Korean War; there were a few more recent monuments to men who died in Vietnam. All of these were interspersed, at peace again, with all the town's civilians.

It was a very solemn kind of game. On finding the grave of a veteran, someone would call out, "Here's one, here's one!" and we'd clear the leaves and branches off, replace last year's little faded American flag with a fresh one, and then read out the name and dates. . . . Before leaving every cemetery, we'd gather in a circle and some child would play "Taps" on the recorder, and someone would read a verse from "Flanders Fields," and then we'd stand in silence (the loud silence of birdsong and spring wind), till the teacher would say so quietly you could barely hear him (he was very shy), "Let us not forget," and we'd move on down the road.

The youngest children with us on those days were remembering things they had not yet even learned, names of people dead in wars they'd never heard of, vast sadnesses their minds could not yet imagine. But even they could grasp it: we were honoring these fallen dead so that someday there would be no more. Together, two dozen souls of mixed age and experience were remembering the future. It was a prayer, though none was spoken.

VICTORIA SAFFORD

Memorial Day Prayer

Spirit of Life
whom we have called by many names in
thanksgiving and in anguish—

Bless the poets and those who mourn
Send peace for the soldiers who did not make the wars
but whose lives were consumed by them

Let strong trees grow above graves far from home
Breathe through the arms of their branches

The earth will swallow your tears while the dead sing
"No more, never again, remember me."

For the wounded ones, and those who received them back,
let there be someone ready when the memories come
when the scars pull and the buried metal moves
and forgiveness for those of us who were not there
for our ignorance.

And in us, veterans in a forest of a thousand fallen
    promises,
let new leaves of protest grow on our stumps.

Give us courage to answer the cry of humanity's pain
And with our bare hands, out of full hearts,
with all our intelligence
let us create the peace.

BARBARA PESCAN

We live in the midst of a great cloud of witnesses, physical ancestors
and spiritual forebears, as well as those whose sacrifices have made
our lives possible. To fail to acknowledge this continuity and our
debt of memory to the dead is to live in a shallow, rootless, and
fleeting present, unconnected to the dignity of our human heritage.

The older we are, the richer and more intricately woven our lives, the more we operate in a community of the living and the dead, whose imperishable memory forms the foundation of our own being. Memorial Day urges us to call these presences explicitly to mind, lest we forget.

KENDYL GIBBONS

It's important to us to remember those who've gone, and why we also want to be remembered. Being remembered is one way to be sure we won't be entirely gone, lost, extinguished. And when we face the death of someone dear to us, whose death means a part of ourself is gone, we may be able to bear it, or accept it, integrate it into our experience a bit better, if we remind ourselves of the person's life, the interactions we had with them, the images which are now part of our memory.

ANNE E. TREADWELL

There is no need to end our relationship with our dead, for they are still ours. Still ours to struggle with, to learn from, and to love. There is no timeline for grieving them and there is no finitude to loving them. Through time—as long a time as it takes—we take their dream and their desires and their issues and integrate them into our own. We make use of whatever hard-won wisdom they were lucky enough to gain while they lived. We continue to forgive them, if forgiveness is called for. We continue the work of their hands.

VICTORIA WEINSTEIN

In this feast of All Souls there is at the very center a great democracy, which leaves none out. We call first to mind our own dead, those whom we have loved and lost but who still live in the twin immensities of our own hearts, our Love and our Memory. But we reach out to others as well, to all whose names live within our memories, whose lives formed the world of our childhood and who have preceded us on life's last journey. Finally we welcome into our loving remembrance those countless men and women and little children who have walked the earth and breathed its air, who have enjoyed the gift of life and known its anxieties, all on every continent and in every time whose individuality has long since disappeared, gathered up in the vast treasury of human life upon this planet. For all have their places on the silent roll of the dead. From this our celebration of All Souls let none be excluded, none forgotten. For every death is in truth a death in the family—in the great human family in which we are all irrevocably bound up with one another.

Death in this past year has taken many whose faces still rejoice our memory's eye, who live still through those of us who loved them.

Death has bound them more closely to us. So it has always been in every year. So will it be next year and in the next—until Death finally visits us as well.

But life itself will remain. As we reflect, in these days of the year's dying, on our own beloved dead, so will others remember us in days to come, until the last days of humankind upon the earth. And even when memory ceases, the substance of our living will still remain, an ineradicable part of what has happened in this corner of the Milky Way.

Max D. Gaebler

On All Souls we remember our beloved dead not as ghosts who haunt, though haunt our imaginations they may, but as members of the Beloved Community whose precious life is Life of our life, Soul of our souls, Heart of our hearts, lingering thought of our minds. We count up the treasures they have left—gifts of life and love and wisdom—and consecrate them to our continued use and progress, that we in our turn may add them to the ever-growing treasures of the common life.

Richard M. Fewkes

O Spirit of Life,
bless us and those who have gone before.
Today we bring memories of loved ones who have died.
Today we share the joys and sorrows that come with the cycle of the
    seasons,
for this is the time to remember, to honor, and to hold the spirits of
    our loved ones.
Breathe into this moment. Know that we are in the company of All
    Saints, All Souls.
Let the presence of those you have loved fill your heart.
Be strengthened by the guiding hand of the grandfathers.
Be nurtured by the compassion of our great grandmothers.
Feel the spirits of the young, who also belong to us.
And be inspired by the vast company of witnesses here gathered.
Let us hold close those who have shown us the way.
May our memories be not a burden of sorrow
but a source of joy and renewed spirit.
For we walk where they have walked
and we carry on their dreams.
May this house be a sanctuary and a resting place.
May it also be a place of preparation—a place to learn
generosity, gentleness, trust, and integrity.
A place to know that we are blessed.

LYNN THOMAS STRAUSS

Do this in remembrance of me.

1 Corinthians 11:24

We light these candles for our families, our beloved ones, and our
    friends,
for those who are near and for those from whom we feel an
    unwanted distance,
for those whose lives are vulnerable,
for our own vulnerable hearts,
for all those we have lost—known and unknown,
for the suffering we have experienced,
for our planet torn by pain.
Let us light these candles in hope and healing.

Hilary Landau Krivchenia

For the Fallen

They shall not grow old, as we that are left grow old;
Age shall not weary them, nor the years condemn.
At the going down of the sun and in the morning
We will remember them.

They mingle not with their laughing comrades again;
They sit no more at familiar tables of home;
They have no lot in our labour of the day-time;
They sleep beyond England's foam.

But where our desires are and our hopes profound,
Felt as a well-spring that is hidden from sight,
To the innermost heart of their own land they are known
As the stars are known to the Night;

As the stars that shall be bright when we are dust,
Moving in marched upon the heavenly plain,
As the stars that are starry in the time of our darkness,
To the end, to the end, they remain.

Lawrence Binyon

A Litany of Remembrance

In the rising of the sun and in its going down, we remember them.

In the blowing of the wind and in the chill of winter, we remember them.

In the opening of buds and in the rebirth of spring, we remember them.

In the blueness of the sky and in the warmth of summer, we remember them.

In the rustling of leaves and in the beauty of autumn, we remember them.

In the beginning of the year and when it ends, we remember them.

When we are weary and in need of strength, we remember them.

When we are lost and sick at heart, we remember them.

When we have joys we yearn to share, we remember them.

So long as we live, they too shall live, for they are now a part of us, as we remember them.

ROLAND B. GITTELSOHN

Oh, may I join the choir invisible
Of those immortal dead who live again
In minds made better by their presence . . .
May I reach
that purest heaven—be to other souls
the cup of strength in some great agony:
enkindle generous ardor, feed pure love,
beget the smiles that have no cruelty;
be the sweet presence of a good diffused,
and in diffusion ever more intense,
So shall I join the choir invisible,
Whose music is the gladness of the world.

GEORGE ELIOT

We die so that the world may continue to live. We have been given the miracle of life because trillions upon trillions of living beings have prepared the way for us and then have died—in a sense, for us. We die, in turn, so that others may live. The tragedy of a single individual becomes, in the balance of natural things, the triumph of ongoing life.

SHERWIN B. NULAND

Days of Memory

These are days of memory.
It has always been so
for our kind
after the leaves have fallen.
The nights are long.
and in the darkness
we remember.

These are days of reflection.
The long, horizontal rays
of the afternoon sun
spill across the earth
with the golden light of memory.

A chilling breeze at twilight
stirs the ground cover of leaves,
stirring also our thoughts.

The elusive beauty of red sunsets
we would hold,
if only we could.

But darkness seeps
from below the horizon.
Day turns into dusk into night.

So we remember.
In our minds,
in the golden light of memory,
we affirm the eternal beauty
of the lives of those who have died
and the goodness of the days that were.

These are days of memory,
of reflection,
of affirmation.
It has always been so for our kind,
after the leaves have fallen.

EDWARD SEARL

They that love beyond the World, cannot be separated by it.

Death cannot kill, what never dies.

Nor can spirits ever be divided that love and live in the same
Divine Principle: the Root and Record of their Friendship.

If Absence be not death, neither is theirs.

Death is but Crossing the World, as Friends do the Seas; They live in one another still.

This is the Comfort of Friends, that though they may be said to Die, yet their Friendship and Society are, in the best Sense, ever present, because Immortal.

WILLIAM PENN

The best tribute we pay to a loved one when she dies is to honestly remember her for the person she was. This is to say about her, yes! You were your own person. You were unique. How you chose to live your life was not without consequence. You mattered. You made a difference for your community, your family, your progeny. Now that your life has ended, we honor the life you chose to live—in all its sparkle and all its shadows. We celebrate your uniqueness. And we freely give you our love, because you gave us life and loved us too.

EDWARD SEARL

Know that the love that blooms inside you is stronger than fear, for people who love find strength they didn't know they had. Know that the love inside you is stronger than illness, for people who love hang in when physical health is gone. And know that love is indeed stronger than death, for people who love are like stones tossed into a pool. The circles of love radiate out and echo back long after the stone has come to rest at the bottom.

MARK DEWOLFE

Jesus was right. Whatever happens to us after we die, life doesn't end in oblivion. It continues in love, our own love, once given, everlasting. Read an obituary unadorned by pretense and your eyes will tell you what your heart already knows.

After death our bodies may be resurrected. Our souls may transmigrate or become part of the heavenly pleroma. We may join our loved ones in Heaven. Or we may return the constituent parts of our being to the earth from which it came and rest in eternal peace. About life after death, no one knows. But about love after death, we surely know. I learned this from my father, as he did from his father and grandfather before him. I learn it also from each of you. The one thing that can never be taken from this world, even by death, is the love we have given away before we die. Those fortunate enough to complete life's seven acts may die sans teeth perhaps, sans eyes, sans taste, sans everything but love. For love, I swear it, is immortal.

FORREST CHURCH

If the dead can come back to this earth and flit
unseen around those they loved, I shall always be near you; in the
garish day and in the darkest night—amidst your happiest scenes and
gloomiest hours—always, always; and if there be a soft breeze
      upon your
cheek, it shall be my breath; or the cool air fans your throbbing
      temple,
it shall be my spirit passing by.

SULLIVAN BALLOU

We emerge from and return to a source, a source that is the stream of life. We are a part of this stream, a part of something much larger than ourselves, and we serve it by the way we live our lives while we are here, and while we are conscious.

We serve that something larger when we recognize and honor all souls as likewise being a part of that grand source of which we are a part. We connect with and serve that something larger, when we celebrate life, even after its passing, by holding in our hearts those who are no longer here, but upon whose shoulders we still stand. We connect with and serve that something larger by honoring those no longer with us, who have taught us, and nurtured us, and led us along the way.

CHARLES BLUSTEIN ORTMAN

Eternal Spirit, we give thanks for all those lives remembered here today. Comfort us when we mourn, and remind us that our tears and our memories are forever sacred. May we remember that "In the evening we may weep, yet joy cometh in the morning." Teach us, O God, to live always with an open heart, for we know that love withdraws when we close our hearts yet ever awaits an open door. O God of Hope, with our hearts open, let us always remember. Amen.

JAN NIELSEN

Between our first cry and our last breath we string together precious moments of life as pearls on a string. Then something or someone breaks the strand and the pearls scatter everywhere. And we are all on our knees on the floor trying to retrieve something that was precious and is now lost. A human life cannot be restrung.

But we can gather together the precious memories in deep gratitude for the time we did have together.

I refuse to believe that either God or the universe is cruel. That is a human failing. Instead I trust that nothing is ever lost. All past and present make up this moment.

LONE I. JENSEN

We are each other's immortality.

Each of us is a skein of lives stretching forward and backward in time, connecting everyone we have known, everyone they have known, and everyone who will come after us. We carry each other back from the threshold of life and death. Some part of those we loved is gone forever, but some part is ours to have and to hold and to make real in the world.

DAVID TAKAHASHI MORRIS

I Am Not Dead

Do not stand at my grave and weep,
I am not there, I do not sleep.

I am a thousand winds that blow.
I am the diamond glint on snow.
I am the sunlight on ripened grain.
I am the gentle autumn rain.

When you wake in the morning hush,
I am the swift, uplifting rush
Of quiet birds, in circling flight.
I am the soft starlight at night.

Do not stand at my grave and weep,
I am not there, I do not sleep.
(Do not stand at my grave and cry.
I am not there, I did not die!)

MARY FRYE

Index of First Lines

Credits

Selections appear on page numbers in bold.

AIKEN   "All Lovely Things Will Have an Ending" (**46**), in *All Lovely Things* by Conrad Aiken, 1916.

ALCOTT   "Transfiguration" (**171**) by Louisa May Alcott, in *A Masque of Poets,* edited by George Parsons Lathrop, 1878.

ANONYMOUS   *Breaking the Silence of Violence* (**154**) by the Committee on the Status of Women in Mission and Ministry, date unknown.

AURELIUS   *Meditations, II* (**11**) by Marcus Aurelius Antoninus, date unknown.

ARENDT   *The Life of the Mind* (**12**) by Hannah Arendt, 1981.

BALDWIN   *The Fire Next Time* (**55**) by James Baldwin, 1963.

BALLOU   Battlefield letter (**196**) by Sullivan Ballou to his wife, 1861.

BARNHOUSE   "Deep Mysteries Have No Words" (**116**), in *Waking Up the Karma Fairy: Life Lessons and Holy Adventures* by Meg Barnhouse, 2003. Used with permission of author.

BARTÓK   Letter (**5**) by Béla Bartók, 1905.

BECKER   *The Denial of Death* (**58**) by Ernest Becker, 1973.

BECKER   Used with permission of Randolph W. B. Becker (**155**).

BELLETINI   Used with permission of Mark Belletini (**43**, **71**).

BENNER   Used with permission of Rebecca F. Benner (**75**).

BERDYAEV   *The Destiny of Man* (**14**, **16**) by Nicholas Berdyaev, translated by Natalie Duddington, 1937.

BERRY   "Ripening" (**60**) by Wendell Berry, in *Collected Poems: 1957–1982*, © 1985. Used with permission of North Point Press, a division of Farrar, Straus and Giroux, LLC.

BERTSCHAUSEN   Used with permission of Roger Bertschausen (**102**).

BINYON   "For the Fallen" (**188**) by Lawrence Binyon, in *The Times*, September 1914.

BLAKE   "Auguries of Innocence" (**66**) by William Blake, in *Life of William Blake* by Alexander Gilchrist, 1863.

BLUEMEL   "Introduction to All Souls" (**113**). Used with permission of Lee Bluemel.

BODEN   Used with permission of Alison L. Boden (**29**).

BOLZ   "Elegy for Thomas Haefemeyer" (**126**). Used with permission of Jody Bolz.

BOOK OF COMMON PRAYER   Burial Service (**47**), *Book of Common Prayer*.

BRONTË   "On The Death of Anne Brontë" (**87**) by Charlotte Brontë, in *Victorian Women Poets*, edited by Angela Leighton, 1995.

BROOKE   "Second Best" (**55**), in *Collected Poems* by Rupert Brooke, 1916.

BROSKIE   Used with permission of Anna Russomano Broskie (**163**).

BUDDHIST BLESSING   "Mythological Themes in Creative Literature and Art" (**107**) by Joseph Campbell, in *Myths, Dreams, and Religions*, edited by Joseph Campbell, 1970.

BUDDHIST PROVERB   Source unknown (**16**).

BUMBAUGH   Used with permission of David E. Bumbaugh (**168**).

BUNAM   Selection (**60**) by Simha Bunam, in *Tales of the Hasidim: The Early Masters* by Martin Buber, translated by Olga Marx, 1961.

BURROUGHS   *Accepting the Universe* (**19**) by John Burroughs, 1920.

ČAPEK   Selection by Norbert Fabian âapek (**37**), in *Norbert Fabian Čapek: A Spiritual Journey* by Richard Henry, 1999.

CARDELL   Selection (**122**) by Nick Cardell used with permission of Cathy Cardell.

CASTANEDA   *Journey to Ixtlan* (**73**) by Carlos Castaneda, 1972.

CAYER   "In Times of Suffering" (**127**). Used with permission of Deborah Cayer.

CHAPIN   Report (**168**) by Augusta Chapin to the Ingham County Historical and Pioneer Society, 1897.

CHUANG TZU   Selection by Chuang Tzu (**14**), in *Chuang Tzu: The Inner Chapters*, translated by David Hinton, 1998.

CHURCH   *Lifecraft* (**13**) by Forrest Church, 2000. "Saving Faith" (**111**). "Love After Death" (**195**) by Forrest Church. Used with permission of author.

COHEN   Used with permission of Helen L. Cohen (**152**).

COHEN   "Good Grief" (**107**). Used with permission of Kenneth L. Cohen.

COIT   *Social Worship* (**89**) by Stanton Coit, 1913.

COLE   "This Many-Splendored Thing" (**130**), in *Give Me No Finished Chants* by Alfred S. Cole, 1968. Used with permission of Bruce Cole.

COLLIER   Used with permission of Kenneth W. Collier (**95**, **147**).

COLLINS   "November" (**69**), in *Sailing Alone Around the Room* by Billy Collins. Copyright © 2001. Used with permission of Random House, Inc.

COOTS   "The Final Time" (**26**), in *Seasons of the Self* by Max A. Coots, 1994. Used with permission of author.

CORINTHIANS   1 Corinthians 11:24 (**188**), King James Version.

COWLEY   "To Dr. Scarborough" (**69**), in *Pindarique Odes* by Abraham Cowley, 1656.

CROSBY   "Beginners" (**26**) and "When the Bottom Falls Out" (**134**), in *Tree and Jubilee* by Greta W. Crosby, 1982. Used with permission of author.

DAVIES   Selection (**125**) by A. Powell Davies in *Great Occasions,* edited by Carl Seaburg, 1968.

DE CHARDIN   "Hymn to Matter" (**21**), in *Hymns of the Universe* by Pierre Teilhard de Chardin, 1961.

DE JONG   Used with permission of Patricia E. de Jong (**35**).

DENNIS   Used with permission of Daniel Dennis (**139**).

DERRIDA   Selection (**46**) by Jacques Derrida, in "Jacques Derrida and Deconstruction" by Mitchell Stephens, in *New York Times Magazine*, January 23, 1994. Used with permission of Mitchell Stephens.

DEWOLFE   Selection (**194**) by Mark DeWolfe used with permission of William A. DeWolfe.

DICKINSON   *Poems* (**56**, **62**, **67**, **92**) by Emily Dickinson, edited by Mabel Loomis Todd and T. W. Higginson, 1890.

DIOP   *Sarzan* (**165**) by Birago Diop, 1955.

DOEGE   Used with permission of Lisa Doege (**135**).

DONNE   *Devotions upon Emergent Occasions* (**54**) by John Donne, 1623.

DOWSON   *Vitae Summa Brevis Spem Nos Vetat Inochare Longam* (**49**) by Ernest Dowson, 1896.

DUNBAR   "The Right to Die" (**146**), in *Selected Poems* by Paul Laurence Dunbar, 1997.

EATON   "A Common Destiny" (**44**) by David Eaton, in *Singing the Living Tradition*, 1993. Used with permission of Dolores P. Eaton.

ECCLESIASTES   Ecclesiastes 7:2-4 (**45**), New Revised Standard Version.

EISELEY   *The Firmament of Time* (**20**) by Loren Eiseley, 1960.

ELIOT   *Adam Bede* (**86**) by George Eliot, 1859. Letter (**96**) by George Eliot, 1878. *Middlemarch* (**175**) by George Eliot, 1900. *The Legend of Jubal and Other Poems* (**191**) by George Eliot, 1874.

EMERSON   Journal (**97**) of Ralph Waldo Emerson, 1842. "Threnody" (**112**), in *Poems* by Ralph Waldo Emerson, 1846. "The Over-soul" (**123**) and "Compensation" (**135**), in *Essays* by Ralph Waldo Emerson, 1841.

EPIC OF GILGAMESH   *The Epic of Gilgamesh* (**90**), translated by N. K. Sanders, 1985.

ERICSSON   *Companion Through Darkness* (**101**) by Stephanie Ericsson, 1993.

ERTZ   *Anger in the Sky* (**11**) by Susan Ertz, 1943.

FEWKES   "All Souls Reflection: On Being Existentially Challenged" (**186**). Used with permission of Richard M. Fewkes.

FOOTE   Selection (**179**) by Arthur Foote used with permission of Frances Foote Stehman.

FOX   "Coping with Grief and Loss" (**99**), inspired by *The Lessons of Loss* by Carol Galginaitis. Used with permission of Ann C. Fox.

FRANKL   *Man's Search for Meaning* (**86**) by Viktor Frankl, 1946.

FRANKLIN   *Poor Richard's Almanac* (**12**) by Benjamin Franklin, 1754.

FRAZIER   *Cold Mountain* (**107**) by Ian Frazier, 1997.

FRIEND   "The Last Year" (**80**), in *Dancing with a Tiger* by Robert Friend. Used with permission of Jean Cantu.

FROMM   *The Sane Society* (**28**) by Erich Fromm, 1955.

FRYE   "I Am Not Dead" (**198**) by Mary Frye, source unknown, 1932.

GAEBLER   Used with permission of Max D. Gaebler (**185**).

GARRETT   Used with permission of Don Garrett (**56**).

GENESIS   Genesis 3:19 (**49**), New Revised Standard Version.

GIBBONS   Used with permission of Kendyl Gibbons (**183**).

GILBERT   "A Tomb Is No Place to Stay" (**138**), in *In the Holy Quiet of This Hour* by Richard S. Gilbert, 1995. Used with permission of author (**36, 138**).

GILMAN   Suicide note by Charlotte Perkins Gilman (**30**), 1935.

GILMORE   "Good-Night" (**93**) by Mary Gilmore, in *An Anthology of Australian Verse,* edited by Bertram Stevens, 2005.

GITTELSOHN   "A Litany of Remembrance" (**189**), in *Gates of Prayer* by Roland B. Gittelsohn, 1975. Used with permission of author.

GOETHE   *Iphigenie* (**19**) by Johann Wolfgang von Goethe, 1787.

GRAHAM   "Meditation" (**27**) by Arthur Graham, in *73 Voices,* edited by Christopher Raible and Edward Darling, 1971. Used with permission of Betty Bippus Graham.

GREDLER   "Jennifer Leigh" (**144**) by Hazel Rogers Gredler, in *Contemporary Accents in Liberal Religion,* selected by Bradford E. Gale, 1960.

GRENFELL   Letter (**141**) by Joyce Grenfell in *Joyce: By Herself and Her Friends,* edited by Reggie Grenfell and Richard Garnett, 1980.

GROSS   Used with permission of Margot Campbel Gross (**109**).

HANH   "Birth and Death" (**51**) and "Oneness" (**150**) by Thich Nhat Hanh, in *Call Me By My True Names.* Used with permission of Parallax Press, Berkeley, California, 1999 (www.parallax.org).

HARDIES   Used with permission of Robert Hardies (**25**).

HARVIE   Used with permission of Kim Crawford Harvie (**121**, **175**).

HAYES   "Love and Remembrance" (**87**, **90**). Used with permission of Mark W. Hayes.

HEAVYSEGE   "The Dead" (**7**) by Charles Heavysege, source unknown.

HEPLER   Used with permission of Kathleen Hepler (**72**).

HERRICK   "All Things Decay and Die" (**44**), in *Works of Robert Herrick*, vol. 1, edited by Alfred Pollard, 1891.

HINDU ASCETIC   *Mysticism* by Evelyn Underhill, 1911 (**4**).

HOLLERORTH   *Death and Immortality: Unitarian and Universalist Views* (**22**) by Barbara Hollerorth, 1986.

HOLM   "The Dead Get By with Everything" (**95**), in *The Dead Get By with Everything*. Minneapolis: Milkweed Editions, 1990. Copyright © 1990 by Bill Holm. Used with permission of Milkweed Editions.

HOLMES   *Address to the Living* (**48**) by John Holmes, 1937. "The Green Door" (**52**) by John Holmes, in *American Poetry Journal,* February 1934. "Death This Year" (**169**) by John Holmes, in *Voices,* February/March 1934. Used with permission of Doris Holmes Eyges.

HOLMES   "The Voiceless" (**18**) by Oliver Wendell Holmes in *Yale Book of American Verse,* edited by Thomas R. Lounsbury, 1912.

HOSMER   "My Dead" (**176**), in *The Thought of God* by Frederick Lucian Hosmer, 1885.

HOWE   Used with permission of Sylvia L'Herrou Howe (**140**).

HUGHES   "Dear Lovely Death" (**123**), in *Dear Lovely Death* by Langston Hughes, 1931.

ICHIKYO   Selection (**67**) by Kozan Ichikyo, in *Japanese Death Poems*, compiled by Yoel Hoffman. Used with permission of Charles E. Tuttle Co., Inc., Boston and Tokyo.

INGERSOLL   *How to Be Saved* (**20**) by Robert Ingersoll, 1880. "At the Grave of a Child" (**137**) by Robert Ingersoll, in *Encyclopedia of Astounding Facts and Useful Information* by Barkham Burroughs, 1889.

JAMES   Diary (**67**) of William James, 1870.

JAPANESE PROVERB   Source unknown (**108**).

JENSEN   Used with permission of Lone I. Jensen (**139**, **197**).

JOHNSON   "Sudden Death and the 'To Do' List" (**59**), in *A Theophany, Please*, 1995. Used with permission of Cynthia B. Johnson.

JOHNSTON   "Life and Death" (**10**), in *Beginning Now: A Book of Explorations* by Donald Johnston, 1970. "Time" (**75**) by Donald Johnston, in *The Tides of Spring and Other Reflections*, edited by Charles W. Grady, 1973.

JONES   Selection (**136**) by Walter Royal Jones, in *Great Occasions*, edited by Carl Seaburg, 1968.

JONG   *Parachutes and Kisses* (**88**) by Erica Jong, 1984.

KAHLO   Diary (**47**) of Frida Kahlo, date unknown.

KEMLER   "Too Close to Death" (**111**), in *How We Are Called*, edited by Mary Benard and Kirstie Anderson, 2002. Used with permission of Elea Kemler.

KENYON   "Notes from the Other Side" (**156**) by Jane Kenyon, copyright © 2005 by the Estate of Jane Kenyon. Reprinted from *Collected Poems* with the permission of Graywolf Press, Saint Paul, Minnesota.

KHAYYAM   *Rubaiyat* (**43**) by Omar Khayyam, translated by Edward Fitzgerald, 1859.

KING   "When I Heard of Your Loss I Called" (**115**), in *How We Are Called*, edited by Mary Benard and Kirstie Anderson, 2002. Used with permission of Pat King.

KINNELL   "Lastness" (**47**), in *The Book of Nightmares* by Galway Kinnell, 1971.

KIRSCHNER   "Three Haiku" (**94**), in *Edges* by Joseph Kirscher, 1999. Used with permission of author.

KRATOCHVIL   Used with permission of Nana Kratochvil (**10**).

KRIVCHENIA   Used with permission of Hilary Landau Krivchenia (**102, 188**).

LANDOR   "Finis" (**18**) by Walter Savage Landor, in *Oxford Book of English Verse, 1250–1900*, edited by Arthur Thomas Quiller-Couch, 1919.

LARKIN   "The Trees" (**158**), in *Collected Poems* by Philip Larkin. Copyright © 1988, 2003 by the Estate of Philip Larkin. Used with permission of Farrar, Straus and Giroux, LLC.

LAWRENCE   "Elegy" (**88**), in *Amores* by D. H. Lawrence, 1916.

LEVERTOV   "Talking to Grief" (**104**) by Denise Levertov, in *Poems 1972–1982*, copyright © 1978 by Denise Levertov. Used with permission of New Directions Publishing Group.

LEVINE   *Who Dies? An Investigation of Conscious Living and Conscious Dying* (**153**) by Stephen Levine, 1982.

LINCOLN   First inaugural speech (**167**) by Abraham Lincoln, 1861.

LOADMAN-COPELAND   Used with permission of Kirk Loadman-Copeland (**85**).

LONGFELLOW   "A Psalm of Life" (**7**) by Henry Wadsworth Longfellow, in *Yale Book of American Verse*, edited by Thomas Raynesford Lonnbury, 1912. "The Reaper and the Flowers" (**48**), in *Voices of the Night* by Henry Wadsworth Longfellow, 1839. "Nature" (**159**), in *The Masque of Pandora* by Henry Wadsworth Longfellow, 1875.

LORDE   "The Transformation of Silence into Language and Action" (**18**), in *Sister Outsider* by Audre Lorde, 1984.

LOWELL   "After the Burial" (**94**), in *Under the Willows and Other Poems* by James Russell Lowell, 1868.

MACLEISH   "The Young Dead Soldiers" (**167**) by Archibald MacLeish, in *Great Occasions,* edited by Carl Seaburg, 1968.

MALLOY   "Epitaph" (**178**), in *My Song for Him Who Never Sang for Me*, 1975. Used with permission of Merrit Malloy.

MANKER-SEALE   Used with permission of Susan Manker-Seale (**24**).

MARKOVA   "I Will Not Die an Unlived Life" (**28**), in *I Will Not Die an Unlived Life* by Dawna Markova, 2000. Used with permission of author. (www.dawnamarkova.com)

MASON AND NOLAN   Used with permission of Dennis E. Mason and Laura Nolan (**165**).

MASTEN   "End Line (for Jim Fulks)" (**81**). Used with permission of Ric Masten (**47, 81**). (www.ric-masten.net)

MASTERS   "The Village Atheist" (**79**), in *Spoon River Anthology* by Edgar Lee Masters, 1916.

MAY   *Freedom and Destiny* (**50**) by Rollo May, 1981. *The Courage to Create* (**69**) by Rollo May, 1975.

MCGEE   "How Do We Face Death?" (**5, 54**). Used with permission of Michael McGee.

MCKEEMAN   "For All Occasions" (**29**), in *Out of the Ordinary* by Gordon B. McKeeman, 2000. Used with permission of author.

MCTIGUE   "They Are With Us Still" (**173**), in *Singing the Living Tradition,* 1993. Used with permission of Kathleen McTigue.

MERWIN   "Separation" (**96**) © 1963 by W. S. Merwin, used with permission of the Wylie Agency Inc. In *The Moving Target* by W. S. Merwin, 1979.

MEYER   Used with permission of Judith E. Meyer (**127**).

MILLER   Used with permission of Beth Miller (**138**).

MILLER   Used with permission of Joel Miller (**3, 6**).

MONROE   "The Cost" (**36**), in *Stopping Places*, edited by Mary Lou Thompson, 1974. Used with permission of Dorothy N. Monroe.

MORRIS   Used with permission of David Takahashi Morris (**198**).

MUIR   *Thousand Mile Walk to the Gulf* (**4**) by John Muir, 1916.

MURFIN   "Introduction to Threnody (To Sandra, Keening the Loss of a Child)" (**112**). Used with permission of Patrick Murfin.

MYSS   *Why People Don't Heal and How They Can* (**127**) by Caroline Myss, 1997.

NIELSEN   Used with permission of Jan Nielsen (**58, 197**).

NIN   *The Diary of Anaïs Nin* (**14**), vol. 2, 1983.

NULAND   *How We Die: Reflections on Life's Final Chapter* (**191**) by Sherwin B. Nuland, 1994.

OLIVER   *The Leaf and the Cloud* (**97**) by Mary Oliver, 2000.

ORR   Selection (**23**) by Hugh Robert Orr, in *A Cup of Strength: Readings in Time of Sorrow and Bereavement*, compiled by Robert Terry Weston, 1945. *Harp of My Heart and Other Poems* (**163**) by Hugh Robert Orr, 1922.

ORTMAN   Used with permission of Charles Blustein Ortman (**196**).

OWL WOMAN   "Death Song" (**62**) by Owl Woman, translated by Francis Densmore, in *Reflections on Wildness*, compiled by Vidyandevi, 2001.

PATTON   "The Affirmation of Death" (**31**), "Autumn Song" (**87**), and "Silent Legend" (**180**) by Kenneth Patton, in *Services and Songs in Celebration of Life* (**3**, **31**, **87**, **167**, **180**), 1967. "Brief Our Days" (39) by Kenneth Patton, in *Hymns for the Celebration of Life*, 1964. Used with permission of Clarise E. Patton.

PAWELEK   Used with permission of Joshua Mason Pawelek (**133**).

PENN   "Union of Friends" (**193**), in *Some Fruits of Solitude* by William Penn, 1909.

PESCAN   "Remembering My Dad" (**86**), "Love Abides" (**144**), "She Speaks of Death" (**149**), and "Memorial Day Prayer" (**182**), in *Morning Watch* by Barbara Pescan, 1999. Used with permission of author.

PETERSBERGER   "Walking Through the Valley of the Shadow" (**128**). Used with permission of Clare L. Petersberger.

PHIFER   "What Does Death Teach Us About Living?" (**76**), in *Hold On: Getting Through Tough Times* by Kenneth W. Phifer, 2001. Used with permission of author.

POTOK   *My Name is Asher Lev* (**72**) by Chaim Potok, 1972.

PRESLEY   Used with permission of Lisa Presley (**105**).

PSALMS   Psalms 90:12 (**43**) and 23 (**130**), King James Version.

QUARLES   "On the World" (**17**) by Francis Quarles, in *Oxford Book of Seventeenth-Century Verse*, edited by H. J. C. Grierson and G. Bullough, 1934.

RANKIN   "Death" (**98**), in *Dancing in the Empty Spaces* by David O. Rankin, 2001. Used with permission of author.

REININGA   "Too Soon" (**91**). Used with permission of Suzanne Reininga.

RENAUD AND RENAUD-EBERLY   Used with permission of Myriam Renaud (**164**).

RINPOCHE   *The Tibetan Book of Living and Dying* (**9**) by Sogyal Rinpoche, 2002.

ROSI-KESSEL   "Crossing Over and Back Again" (**34**). Used with permission of Rachele Rosi-Kessel.

ROSSETTI   "Remember Me" (**108**), in *Questions About Angels* by Christina Rossetti, 1862. "Song" (**141**), in *Goblin Market and Other Poems* by Christina Rossetti, 1862.

ROWE   Used with permission of Jean M. Rowe (**125**).

RZEPKA   "On Being Scared" (**116**), in *A Small Heaven* by Jane Rzepka, 1989. Used with permission of author.

SAFFORD   "Set in Stone" (**23**), "In Between" (**38**), "Credo for Now" (**52**), and "Memory" (**181**), in *Walking Toward Morning* by Victoria Safford, 2003. Used with permission of author (**23, 38, 52, 117, 181**).

SAINT-ÉXUPÉRY   *Wind, Sand, and Stars* (**46**) by Antoine de Saint-Éxupéry, translated by Lewis Galantière, 1939.

SANDBURG   "Stars, Songs, Faces" (**124**), in *Smoke and Steel* by Carl Sandburg, 1920.

SANTAYANA   "To W. P. II" (**91**) by George Santayana and "To W. P. I" (**168**) by George Santayana, in *Great Occasions*, edited by Carl Seaburg, 1968. *Introduction to Spinoza's Ethics* (**170**) by George Santayana, 1910.

SARTON   "All Souls" (**65**), in *Selected Poems* by May Sarton, edited by May Sarton and Serena S. Hilsinger, 1978. *After the Stroke* (**153**) by May Sarton, 1988.

SCHMITZ   Used with permission of Kathryn A. Schmitz (**174**).

SCOTT   "Memory" (**177**), in *Promise of Spring* by Clinton Lee Scott, 1977. Used with permission of Peter Lee Scott.

SCOTT   "Gypsy Song" (**176**). Used with permission of Marylyn Motherbear Scott.

SEARL   *In Memoriam: Modern Funeral and Memorial Services* (**74**) by Edward Searl, 2000. "Days of Memory" (**191**), in *A Place of Your Own* by Edward Searl, 1998.

SENRYU   Selection (**63**) by Senryu, in *Japanese Death Poems*, compiled by Yoel Hoffman. Used with permission of Charles E. Tuttle Co., Inc., of Boston and Tokyo.

SEWELL   Used with permission of Marilyn Sewell (**116**).

SHAKESPEARE   *Hamlet* (**43**) by William Shakespeare, 1603. "Sonnet 73" (**61**) and "Sonnet 3" (**109**), in *The Oxford Shakespeare*, edited by W. J. Craig, 1914. *Julius Caesar* (**68**) by William Shakespeare, 1623. *MacBeth* (**86**) by William Shakespeare, 1606. *Richard III* (**90**) by William Shakespeare, c. 1591.

SHAW   "Dedicatory Letter" (**12**), in *Man and Superman* by George Bernard Shaw, 1903.

SIBR   "As the World Spins Around" (**21**). Used with permission of Carolyn J. Sibr.

SIMONS   Used with permission of Grace H. Simons (**122**).

SOELLE   "Suffering" (**105**) by Dorothee Soelle, in *Tree and Jubilee*, edited by Greta W. Crosby, 1982.

SOUTHWORTH   *This Day: Worship Resources for the Liberal Church* (**117**) by Bruce Southworth, 1987. Used with permission of author.

SPENDER   "I Think Continually of Those Who Were Truly Great" (**173**), in *Poems* by Stephen Spender, 1933.

STEGNER   *Crossing to Safety* (**19**) by Wallace Stegner, 1987.

STEVENS   "Sunday Morning" (**9**) by Wallace Stevens, in *The New Poetry: An Anthology*, edited by Harriet Monroe, 1917.

STEVENSON   Eulogy for Eleanor Roosevelt (**52**) by Adlai Stevenson, in *Farewell, Godspeed: The Greatest Eulogies of Our Time,* edited by Cyrus M. Copeland, 2003.

STRAUBE   Used with permission of Arvid Straube (**170**).

STRAUSS   Used with permission of Lynn Thomas Strauss (**51, 187**).

SWINBURNE   "The Garden of Proserpine" (**13**), in *Poems and Ballads* by Algernon Charles Swinburne, 1866.

TABB   "Life Again" (**155**) by John Banister Tabb, in *Singing the Living Tradition,* 1993.

TAGORE   *Sadhana: The Realisation of Life* (**124**) by Rabindranath Tagore, 1916.

TARBOX   "All Is Dukkha" (**64**), in *Life Tides*, 1993. Used with permission of Sarah Tarbox for the estate of Elizabeth Tarbox.

TAVES   Used with permission of Krista Taves (**111**).

TEASDALE   "Alchemy" (**132**), in *Rivers to the Sea* by Sara Teasdale, 1915.

TENNYSON   *In Memoriam* (**156**) by Alfred Lord Tennyson, 1850.

THOREAU   *A Week on the Concord and Merrimack Rivers* (**166**) by Henry David Thoreau, 1849.

THURMAN   *Meditations of the Heart* (**106**) by Howard Thurman, copyright © 1953, 1981 by Anne Thurman. Reprinted with permission of Beacon Press, Boston.

TRAPP   "Thoughts for Meditation" (**32**), edited by Jacob Trapp, *The Unitarian Register*, March 1957. Selection (**70**) found among Jacob Trapp's papers after his death. "Thoughts for Meditation" (**98**), edited by Jacob Trapp, *The Unitarian Register*, date unknown. Used with permission of John C. Trapp on behalf of Helen Trapp.

TREADWELL   Used with permission of Anne E. Treadwell (**184**).

TYNDALL   Used with permission of Ann E. Tyndall (**71**).

VAN GOGH   Selection (**121**) by Vincent Van Gogh, in *The Complete Letters of Vincent van Gogh*, edited by Robert Harrison and translated by Johanna van Gogh-Bonger, 1991.

VORIES   "Life Is Too Brief" (**66**) by M. Vories, in *A Cup of Strength: Readings in Time of Sorrow and Bereavement*, compiled by Robert Terry Weston, 1945.

WALLER   "Of the Last Verses in the Book" (**33**), in *Poems* by Edmund Waller, 1686.

WEINSTEIN   Used with permission of Victoria Weinstein (**172**, **184**).

WELLS   *The Strangeness of This Business* (**133**) by Clark Dewey Wells, 1975. Used with permission of author

WESTON   "Out of Clouds and Sunshine" (**48**), "Autumn Speaks" (**157**), and "The Great Peace" (**142**), in *Seasons of the Soul* by Robert T. Weston, 1963. *A Cup of Strength: Readings in Time of Sorrow and Bereavement* (**116**), compiled by Robert T. Weston, 1945. Selection (**136**) by Robert T. Weston, in *Life Prayers: 365 Prayers, Blessings, and Affirmations to Celebrate the Human Journey*, edited by Elizabeth Roberts and Elias Amidon, 1996. "This Is the Truth That Passes Understanding" (**139**) by Robert T. Weston, in *Singing the Living Tradition*, 1993. Selection (**143**) by Robert T. Weston, in *Memorial Services for Women*, edited by Meg Bowman, 1984. Used with permission of Richard Weston-Jones.

WHEAT   *In Pursuit of Joy* (**89**, **97**) by Donald H. Wheat, 1994.

WHEELOCK   "Life" (**60**) by John Hall Wheelock, in *The Little Book of Modern Verse*, edited by Jessie B. Rittenhouse, 1917.

WHITE   "Youth and Age" (**64**) by E. B. White, source unknown. Used with permission of Colleen M. White.

WHITMAN   *Leaves of Grass* (**14**) by Walt Whitman, c. 1900.

WHITNEY   "In Spring" (**22**) by George C. Whitney, in *The Tides of Spring and Other Reflections*, edited by Charles Wesley Grady, 1973.

WILDE   "Necessary Losses" (**50**). Used with permission of Sydney K. Wilde.

WILDER   *Our Town* (**123**) by Thornton Wilder, 1938. *Bridge of San Louis Rey* (**145**) by Thornton Wilder, 1927.

WILLIAMS   "Foreword" to *The Rose Tattoo* (**70**) by Tennessee Williams, 1951.

WOLFE   "Some Things Will Never Change" (**49**), in *The Web and the Rock* by Thomas Wolfe, 1937. *You Can't Go Home Again* (**55**) by Thomas Wolfe, 1934.

WOOD   "Many Winters" (**31**), in *Many Winters* by Nancy Wood, Doubleday & Co., © 1972. All rights reserved. Used with permission of Nancy Wood.

WORDSWORTH   "Ode on Intimations of Immortality" (**148, 151**), in *The Complete Poetical Works* by William Wordsworth, 1888.

YEVTUSHENKO   "People" (**93**) by Yevgeny Yevtushenko, source unknown.

YORK   *Remembering Well: Rituals for Celebrating Life and Mourning Death* (**103**) by Sarah York, 2000. "Forgiveness" (**147**), in *Into the Wilderness* by Sarah York, 1990. Used with permission of author.

ZOLL   "To Fill the Void" (**148**), in *How We Are Called*, edited by Mary Benard and Kirstie Anderson, 2002. Used with permission of Mary Zoll.